A Coastal Companion

A YEAR IN THE GULF OF MAINE, FROM CAPE COD TO CANADA

Catherine Schmitt

Illustrated by
Kimberleigh Martul-March
and
Margaret Campbell

Tilbury House, Publishers
8 Mechanic Street
Gardiner, Maine 043345
800–582–1899 • www.tilburyhouse.com

First paperback edition: April 2008
10 9 8 7 6 5 4 3 2 1

Library of Congress Cataloging-in-Publication Data
Schmitt, Catherine, 1976-
    A coastal companion : a year in the Gulf of Maine, from Cape Cod to
Canada / by Catherine Schmitt. — 1st pbk. ed.
        p. cm.
    Includes bibliographical references and index.
    ISBN 978-0-88448-303-8 (pbk. : alk. paper)
    1. Coastal ecology—Maine, Gulf of. 2. Natural history—Maine, Gulf of.
3. Coastal ecology—Atlantic Coast (Canada) 4. Natural history—
Atlantic Coast (Canada) I. Title.
    QH104.5.M24.S36 2008
    508.74—dc22   2007047093

Cover illustration by by Kimberleigh Martul-March
Copyediting Genie Dailey, Fine Points Editorial Services, Jefferson, Maine.
Printed and bound by

We crave the verse that shall give us
     the taste of salt spray upon our lips.

— John Burroughs

ABOUT MAINE SEA GRANT

The Maine Sea Grant College Program is part of a national network of thirty programs of the National Oceanic and Atmospheric Administration (NOAA). Working in partnership with marine industries, scientists, government agencies, private organizations, municipalities, Maine residents and visitors, Maine Sea Grant supports marine science research and outreach activities to promote the understanding, sustainable use, and conservation of the state's marine and coastal resources. Maine Sea Grant supports local artists as part of a broader effort to preserve the heritage of Maine's coastal communities.

ACKNOWLEDGMENTS

First, I must give credit for the idea for this book to Susan White, Associate Director at Maine Sea Grant. This book could not have happened without her encouragement and support, which took many forms. Thanks to Susan, also, for her careful editing of the manuscript in its final stages. Thanks to everyone at Maine Sea Grant, especially Beth Owen, for help with background research, and to Natalie Springuel and Paul Anderson for contributing ideas and their extensive knowledge of the Gulf of Maine.

Special thanks to Kathleen Ellis for helping to identify and contact Maine poets, and to Sanford Phippen for showing me the world of Maine literature. I am indebted to all the poets who submitted work; their enthusiasm became my motivation.

Several people reviewed sections for scientific accuracy, including Joseph Kelley, Brian Beal, Katherine Webster, Jim McCleave, and Sea Grant Marine Extension Team members Natalie Springuel, Chris Bartlett, and Dana Morse. The staff and resources at the Raymond H. Fogler Library at the University Maine, in particular Special Collections, were invaluable.

The understanding of my coworkers at the Senator George J. Mitchell Center for Environmental and Watershed Research allowed me to spend more time on this project. Thanks to the artists, Margaret Campbell and Kim Martul-March, for their patience and willingness to accompany me on this journey through the Gulf of Maine.

Recognition is due to Murray and Ted, for their guidance, and to Eric, thank you.

Catherine Schmitt
Orono, Maine

FOR A NEW NEW YEAR'S MORNING

Sun-swell down and east
from Great Pond Mountain
is an ocean of coming up light. Night
an ebbing tide with shoresong
sure as any. Our woodlot-top a coast

to an inland miraging sea. Day a rising bay
so fluid lobster boats could haul traps from it
on lines dripping with freezing salt.
That black fir spire could be a steeple
crackling over a town tucked around ice-

bound cove. Those flat-bottomed clouds: islands
fast as Mount Desert under snow. See
how first light gives new dreams
through old growth pine. An ocean
needs only to be wished for; conjured,

any sea can be. Dawn washes
the waking pasture flooding on
to become its own day. You'd never know
the Atlantic breaks outback each sunreach
unless as I do, you believe.

Patricia Ranzoni
Bucksport, Maine

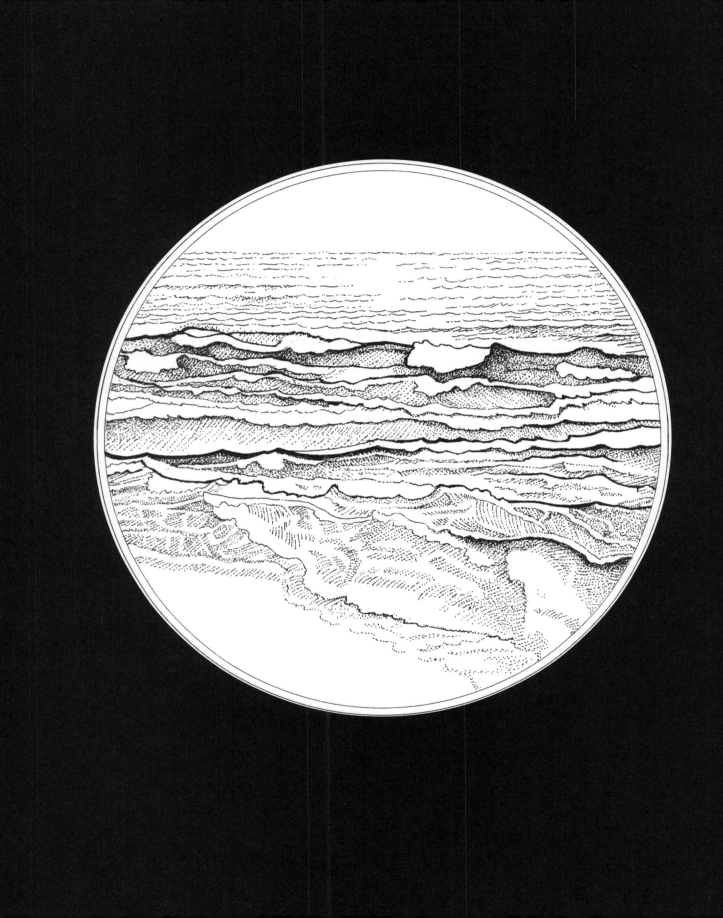

January

January 1

On this New Year's Day, a day of beginnings, let us begin with the ocean. The ocean is the origin of all life on earth—we came from the ancient sea that once covered the planet, and still carry with us remnants of its salt. As President John F. Kennedy observed in 1962, "It is an interesting biological fact that all of us have, in our veins, the exact same percentage of salt in our blood that exists in the ocean, and, therefore, we have salt in our blood, in our sweat, in our tears. We are tied to the ocean. And when we go back to the sea, whether it is to sail or to watch— we are going back from whence we came."

To begin, then, the sea.

January 2

The word *ocean* is from the Greek *okeanos*, "a river encircling the earth," and is derived from the ancient Sanskrit term for "encircling all around." The name is apt, as oceans flow in a circulation pattern not unlike a river. Cold, sinking water flows east above Antarctica, north along Australia toward the Bering Strait and Alaska, then loops back south along the West Coast of the U.S., across the Indian Ocean and along the west coast of Africa and Europe into the North Atlantic, where it influences the Gulf of Maine. The "conveyor belt" then turns south, grazing Newfoundland and crossing the Gulf Stream before flowing along South America until the circulation is complete.

The river encircling the earth is but one ocean that is constantly moving, interacting with the atmosphere to drive the earth's climate. The ocean absorbs energy from the sun and stores it as heat. The ocean absorbs more heat than land since it occupies nearly three-quarters of the planet. As wind drives the currents that propel the ocean's circulation around the globe, heat is also carried along from the tropics to the northern latitudes. Eventually, heat escapes from the ocean in the form of rain and storms. In this complicated dance of water, wind, sun, and sky, the ocean transports the sun's energy around the world and so maintains the earth's temperature.

January 3

Here on the first nights of the year, when the mountains are darker than the sky and the sky is darker than the sea, it is hard to believe that our planet is actually closest to the sun. This moment, called perihelion, occurs during the first week in January, after the winter solstice. This thought is bare solace to those of us in the Northern Hemisphere, who now lean away from the sun. Greater hope might be found in the fact that these days are gaining light, as our home ground slowly tilts back toward the great star.

January 4

Artist and poet Marsden Hartley was born in Lewiston, Maine, on this day in 1877. One of America's greatest modernist painters, Hartley learned and practiced his talents all over the U.S. and abroad, and became known for his dramatic use of color and thick layering of paint. Hartley finally returned to Maine at age sixty, and published *Androscoggin*, his second volume of poems. He wrote of change, and coming home, as in this passage from "Return of the Native":

> *He who finds will*
> *to come home*
> *will surely find old faith*
> *made new again*
> *and lavish welcome.*

January 5

Our part of the global ocean is the Atlantic, which takes its name from *Ocean of the Atlanteans*, the one great ocean of the ancients. The name first appeared in the writings of Herodotus 7,000 years ago, and refers to the Atlas mountains in northwest Africa (themselves named after the god Atlas), which the ancient Greeks believed overlooked the entire ocean. Greek mythology contains numerous references to the sea. Poseidon was the god of the sea, brother of Zeus who ruled the sky and Hades who ruled the underworld. There were sirens, tritons, and Proteus, who guarded Poseidon's herd of seals. In Norse myth, Aegir was the god of the seashore and ocean.

January 6

Within the northwestern Atlantic Ocean, the Gulf of Maine is a semienclosed sea bounded to the north by Nova Scotia and New Brunswick, on the west by the coasts of Maine, New Hampshire, and Massachusetts, to the south by the cradled arm of land that is Cape Cod, and on the east by the shallow shoals of Georges Bank and Browns Bank. These banks limit water exchange with the open Atlantic, which must rush into the Gulf through the Northeast Passage, a deep, narrow channel that runs between the banks. Water entering the 36,000-square-mile Gulf of Maine is flung northeastward by the force of the spinning earth toward Nova Scotia and the Bay of Fundy, then flows counterclockwise along the New England coast before exiting through the Great South Channel between western Georges Bank and Nantucket Shoals. A single revolution around the Gulf takes three months—each season, the water in the Gulf is renewed, always moving, always changing, following the turn of the earth and the tide of time.

January 7

Look out across the cold, steel ocean. The ocean never sleeps, for beneath the waves a diverse ecosystem is churning with life, no matter the season. Marine environments become more diverse as the water gets colder, unlike land-based ecosystems which tend to have greater biological diversity in warmer climates— think of the rainforests of South and Central America. And so the cold waters of the Gulf of Maine are some of the world's most productive, providing habitat for over 3,300 marine species, including 652 different kinds of fish, 184 species of birds, and 32 species of mammals, according to the Census of Marine Life, a ten-year initiative to document the diversity of life in the oceans.

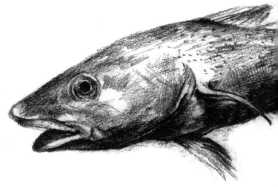

cod

January 8

Much of this varied marine life has provided sustenance to people around the world for centuries. Today, seafood remains a crucial part of the daily diet for residents of countries without other sources of local protein. Almost half of the world's population relies on the sea for at least 20 percent of their animal protein, and some small island nations depend on fish almost exclusively. About 57 percent of our total food-fish supply is obtained from fishing in marine and inland waters; the remaining amount is produced via aquaculture. The Gulf of Maine is a major source of seafood: each year, commercial fishermen in Maine, Massachusetts, and New Hampshire harvest over 600 million pounds of fish and shellfish from Gulf waters.

January 9

In the winter, the windswept shore can seem blank, the waves barren. Most fish and even lobsters have left for warmer waters to the south or the deeper basins in the outer Gulf. But one of the Gulf's prize seafood species, the Atlantic cod (*Gadus morhua*), begins moving closer to shore to begin spawning from now until spring. In Ipswich and Massachusetts bays, cod spawn from December to February, and there are fall spawning populations in Canadian waters, although the majority of spawning in the Gulf occurs in March. After arriving at their respective spawning areas, Atlantic cod often gather into large schools near the sea bottom. They are broadcast spawners, which means males release their sperm into the water in close proximity to females, who can release up to nine million eggs in a single spawning. Larvae will grow into juveniles, and at the end of their first year in the North Atlantic they will be about six inches long. It is difficult to overestimate the role of Atlantic cod in the colonial history of New England and the Canadian Maritimes. The cod was so important to New England's early economy that a carved wooden cod was hung in the Massachusetts House of Representatives in Boston. Stocks of the fish in the Gulf of Maine collapsed in the early 1990s due to overfishing, and today fishermen are working with scientists to bring them back.

January 10

Unaffected by the ice and wind, some organisms like cod have evolved to cope with cold and saltier seas. Intertidal organisms that are mobile relocate to higher-salinity tide pools or, like periwinkles, migrate down the tide line to reduce the amount of time they are exposed to the cold air. Snails and crabs seek shelter under seaweeds or rocks. Seaweeds and animals that are immobile are dark in color and absorb solar radiation from the noonday sun to stay warm. Some fishes, including the Atlantic cod, tomcod, short-horned sculpin (*Myoxocephalus scorpius*), and winter flounder, have "antifreeze" in their blood. These fish produce molecules of salt and protein that lower the freezing point of their body fluids, making it possible for them to stay in colder near-shore waters. Seaweeds, mussels, and some fish can increase the salt content of their body fluids by either losing water or taking in salt; as in the ocean itself, this higher salt content helps to prevent freezing.

January 11

How cold does the ocean have to be before it freezes? The freezing point of seawater depends on its salinity, the amount of salt in the water. The saltier the water, the colder it has to be for it to freeze. Ocean water, which has 35 parts salt for every thousand parts water (35 ppt salinity) will freeze at 28.4°F (-2°C). Salt interferes with the water's ability to form ice crystals by blocking and surrounding the water molecules. Amid all that salt, it takes longer for water molecules to "find each other" and freeze together, and when they do, the salt tends to stay behind in the liquid water. Ice has no room for salt. The resulting brine gets saltier and saltier and freezes even more slowly at colder temperatures. You'd have to go to the Arctic to see real frozen sea ice; it simply is not cold enough in the Gulf of Maine. Instead, slush piles up on the shores of bays and inlets, granules of ice mixing with foam in the green brine. The high tide sloshes against rocks and cliffs, making a percussive sound like rain, or brushes on a drum.

January 12

In addition to delaying the freezing process, salt also makes seawater heavier and more dense than pure water. In an estuary, where the ocean tides push inland and rivers flow toward the sea, the outgoing fresh river water floats on top of the heavier, incoming marine water. In addition, warm water expands (water molecules drift away from each other) and is less dense, or lighter, than cold water. Warm seawater always floats on top of cold seawater until the ocean is mixed by turbulence, waves, or other disturbance. This difference in density, driven by temperature and salinity, is an important factor in ocean circulation.

January 13

The ice and snow that surround us this time of year bring a shuddering chill in the bones, waking a memory carried from our human ancestors who witnessed glaciers moving across North America. During the last Ice Age 25,000 years ago, the great Laurentide ice sheet covered New England. The edge of the glacier pushed piles of sand, rock, and debris that became Nantucket and Martha's Vineyard, Massachusetts. Then, as the ice retreated year after year, the sea followed, reaching far up the Kennebec and Penobscot river valleys in Maine, flooding the land. Marine silt and clay, as well as shells and other bits of animals settled to the sea bottom. On Cape Cod, the ocean formed salt marshes and beaches. Finally, freed from the weight of the glaciers, the land began to rebound and the ocean receded, eventually settling close to current sea level. Remains from this postglacial sea can still be found today: fossils in the marine clay sediments along the coast. Saltwater peat from the Great Marshes in Barnstable County, Massachusetts, is 5,480 years old.

Short-Horned Sculpin

Sandworm

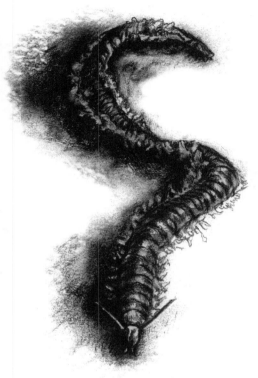

January 14

As the ice advanced and retreated across the continental edge, gravel, stones, and boulders that were trapped beneath the ice were ground into the bedrock, forming grooves and gouges in granite. Softer rock was washed away and the coast of northern New England became the "ragged sleeve" we know today. "The whole coastline appears as though it had been 'combed' down into the sea," wrote John Kingsbury in *The Rocky Shore*. The comb might have been a sheet of ice 1,000 feet thick. In other parts of Maine and New England, the coast is softer. Waves gnaw at bluffs of loose-packed sand and currents carve the shore into bays and sandy beaches. In northeastern Massachusetts and parts of Cape Cod, strands of dunes on barrier islands take the brunt of the ocean's force, as marshes form in quieter waters behind the beaches. All of these coastal landforms are evolving, as sand drifts away, granite slowly erodes, bluffs crumble into the waves, and storm surges break through the dunes to create new inlets.

January 15

With most predators far out to sea for the winter, those animals that remain in estuaries can venture out from their hiding places. On an ebbing tide under cover of winter's night, sandworms leave their sandy burrows to swim about at the water's surface. *Nereis virens* are a popular bait for saltwater anglers and a food for cultured fish and shrimp. Sandworms can reach great lengths, sometimes exceeding four feet, but those used for bait are much smaller. Along both sides of their bodies are many small legs which technically are not legs at all but parapodia, external gills that also help the worm move around. Ranging in color from reddish-brown to green, sandworms (also called clam worms) have blue heads with two large, nasty pincer teeth that they will use on humans.

January 16

In January, there is a chance of spotting gray seals, or horseheads, which bear young in winter. In Maine, gray seal pups are born between December and February in Penobscot and Frenchman bays. Gray seals (*Halichoerus grypus*) are much larger and less common than harbor seals, which also are present in winter. In addition, harp, hooded, ringed, and bearded seals—the ice seals—wander south this time of year. Wounded or otherwise unhealthy seals may strand on beaches or come close to shore, requiring rescue by members of the marine mammal stranding network. Remember that seals are wild animals and should not be approached or harassed in any way. If you think a seal is in danger, do not touch it or attempt to help it; instead, call Allied Whale at College of the Atlantic in Bar Harbor, Maine, or the New England Aquarium in Boston.

Harbor Seals

January 17

On those days when the coast is empty save for shades of blue and gray, when seals and swimming worms are nowhere to be found, a walk through a coastal forest reveals a palette of greens unseen in other seasons. Without competition from the tender, almost neon green of spring, or the lush overlapping leaf-green of summer, mosses and lichens and evergreens stand out, or perhaps are sought after by eyes tired of staring at a clean slate. Black-green spruces and soft pines and bright firs separate into subtle shades, sometimes the only color in January's winter wonderland. These evergreens have adapted over thousands of years to life in the presence of cold and snow. The spires of black and red spruce stand out against the lighter greens of pine, hemlock, fir, and cedar. Hormones prevent the branches from growing out horizontally, and the result is the narrow, pointed shape of spruce and fir, perhaps an adaptive strategy in heavy snow country.

Balsam Fir

Birches, too, have grown to live with winter. A black-and-white etching upon the blank landscape, their trunks bend beneath the weight of snow and ice, as observed by Robert Frost:

When I see birches bend to left and right
      Across the lines of straighter darker trees,
            I like to think some boy's been swinging them.
      But swinging doesn't bend them down to stay
            As ice-storms do.

Frost was likely writing about gray birches, which are the most flexible of the northern birches. Gray birches (*Betula populifolia*) have chalky bark that does not peel, with black chevrons, triangle-shaped markings, on their trunks. They grow in clearings, old fields, and burned areas. White or paper birches look similar to gray birches, but their white, peeling bark separates into papery layers, and the trunks have thin dark horizontal lines. Native Americans found white birches growing along streams or bordering lakes and ponds, and used the peeling bark to make canoes, boxes, cups, and other items. Crowning coastal hills and lining the banks of icy mountain streams alongside hemlocks is the yellow or silver birch, the largest of our native birches. Black or sweet birch is found only in the southern Gulf of Maine region. Break a twig from a black or yellow birch for a hint of wintergreen oil. On coastal headlands and islands east of Mount Desert Island grows the mountain paper birch, a natural hybrid with reddish-brown or white peeling bark.

Birches

Birches Bent by Snow

12

January 19

"Oh, horror upon horror! the ice opens suddenly…and we are whirling dizzily, in immense concentric circles, round and round the borders of a gigantic amphitheatre, the summit of whose walls is lost in the darkness.…
But little time will be left me to ponder upon my destiny…we are plunging madly within the grasp of the whirlpool and amid a roaring, and bellowing, and shrieking of ocean and of tempest, the ship is quivering,
oh God! and going down."

So wrote Edgar Allen Poe, who was born on this day in 1809 in Boston, Massachusetts. Poe has been described as brilliant and unstable, a romantic poet, a master of macabre tales, and the originator of the modern detective story. In this passage from *Tales of the Grotesque and Arabesque*, Poe describes what it might be like to get caught in a frozen whirlpool, perhaps even the "Old Sow," the largest ocean whirlpool in the Western Hemisphere and the second largest in the world. Whirlpools are formed where opposing currents and tides meet; the Old Sow is created by currents from the St. Croix River mixing with tidal waters between Eastport, Maine, and Deer Island, New Brunswick. An undersea mountain and several deep trenches in the Western Passage enhance the formation of the Old Sow vortex, which can grow as large as 250 feet in diameter and spins off smaller whirlpools, locally called "piglets."

Stoneflies

January 20

Where birches bend over cool, unfrozen streams, winter stoneflies are hatching. Winter stoneflies are small, less than one inch long, and shiny black or dark brown. Look for them walking on the snow, basking on bridges and fenceposts, and on tree trunks along the sunlit banks of clear, cold, well-oxygenated streams. Stoneflies are sensitive to pollution, and their presence is an indicator of good water quality. In late winter, the young nymphs climb out of the water and shed their skins, becoming adults. They will feed for awhile on dead plant material and algae, and then enter a hibernation-like state until the fall.

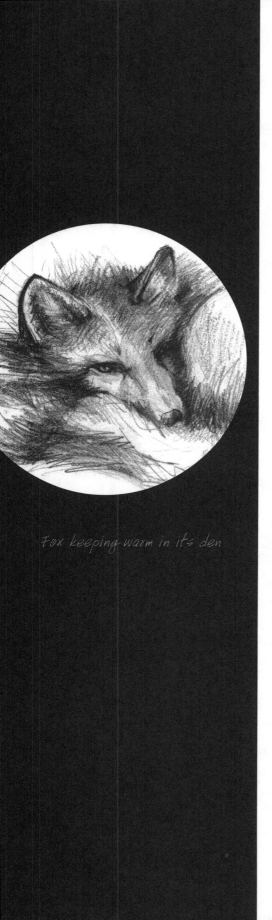

Stoneflies and other insects like mayflies and dragonflies are primitive creatures, originating during the era of the dinosaurs. They are some of the few animals and plants that survived the Ice Age and the melting of glaciers, when rivers found new channels and the Atlantic Ocean moved inland. Sturgeon, horseshoe crabs, and snapping turtles also have prehistoric lineage, as do ferns and mosses and some trees.

January 21
Animals that are more recent inhabitants of today's coast have had to evolve ways to keep warm in winter. They huddle together, which reduces the amount of surface area exposed to the cold, or modify their environment by building protective nests or burrowing into the "subnivean" world beneath the snow. Mice and voles that are solitary during the summer will congregate during the winter in communal nests. Birds fluff their feathers to make insulating layers of air between their bodies and the cold. Other animals just shiver: when not flying, crows and ravens shiver continuously during the winter to maintain body heat.

Other mammals and birds remain active in the winter, and the bright, slanting morning sun of these lengthening days is perfect light for finding signs of their activity. Most of the time when walking outside we have little idea of the animals that have come before us on the trail. But in winter, their tracks are left in the snow and we can see how crowded a place really is. Even the tiniest mouse will leave a shadowy stitch across smooth snow. The intaglio of feathers in snow where wingtips brush the earth marks a brief meeting of sky and land. Tracks take experience and a good guidebook to identify, but they are just as intriguing when left a mystery.

January 22

Animal tracks in the snow are especially prominent in the bluish glow of moonlight, and a winter full moon would invite us to strap on snowshoes and tread silently across the frozen landscape. The first full moon of the year is the Hunger Moon or Wolf Moon, named for the wolf packs howling in the cold deep midwinter snows. Full moon names originated in Native American cultures of northeastern North America; tribes kept track of the seasons by giving distinctive names to each full moon. This time of year was a lean one for Native people, as food stocks dwindled and deep snows made hunting and gathering difficult. Wolves, too, grew hungry, their pangs echoing out across the snow and sky beneath a silver-white moon. Eastern timber wolves once occupied the northeastern United States, including all of New England and New York, and still exist in Canada to the north and west.

Mice and Hare Tracks

January 23

The moon and the sea have long been paired in history and folklore, with good reason. The moon is the dominant force influencing the tides, and so lunar phases and tidal rhythms wax and wane, ebb and flow in synchronicity. The tides have been cause for wonder since the earliest humans. Early Asian and Arabic cultures, and later Greek and Roman philosophers, attempted to explain the tides. But it was not until Isaac Newton showed that the gravitational forces of the moon varied over the surface of the earth that scientists widely believed that it was the moon that influenced the tides. The word *tide* derives from the Anglo-Saxon tyd which means "seasons."

January 24

In the Northern Hemisphere, January is on average the coldest month. But a spike in temperatures above freezing, often during the third week of the month, is the phenomenon of "January thaw." While there is dispute over whether or not the thaw really exists, New England folklore and scientific data suggest that it is real. But who really cares if the thaw is statistically proven? Any increase in temperature, and the hope and relief that come with it, is welcome at this time of year. Aldo Leopold wrote in *A Sand County Almanac*, "Each year, after the midwinter blizzards, there comes a night of thaw when the tinkle of dripping water is heard in the land. It brings strange stirrings, not only to creatures abed for the night, but to some who have been asleep for the winter." January thaw helps to wake us from a winter haze, reminding us that the world is alive, and so are we.

January 25

Look up. Soaring above the bare peninsulas of the Northeastern coast are increasing numbers of bald eagles. Tens of thousands leave their northern breeding areas to spend the winter in the continental U.S. The bald eagle (*Haliaeetus leucocephalus*) is also known as the American eagle, since it occurs only in North America. It is essentially a fishing eagle, and therefore is typically seen near seacoasts, large rivers, and lakes. During the breeding season eagles are territorial, but in the winter they roost and hunt in groups. Along the Merrimack River, Massachusetts, Great Bay, New Hampshire, and the large tidal rivers of the Maine coast, bald eagles are feeding where the water is free of ice. The eagle's white head and tail is more striking now when the contrast is mirrored by the landscape; these white feathers are the origin of the eagle's name, which comes from the Old English word balde, meaning white. The white head and tail are indicative of a mature eagle that is at least five years old.

Gyrfalcon

January 26

Some birds are associated with winter or snow and ice in folklore. The gyrfalcon, the largest falcon that is occasionally spotted in winter, is called the ice falcon in Nova Scotia. The glaucous gull, also called the ice gull, is a large, pale arctic gull that winters in the Northeast, mingling with other gulls at garbage dumps and harbors, or seeking food further out to sea. Glaucous gulls are quite similar to Iceland gulls but are larger, have larger bills and flatter heads, and, at rest, have shorter wingtips that barely project beyond the end of the tail. Both can be distinguished from the common herring gull, which has black wingtips.

Common Eider

January 27

As naturalist John Burroughs said, "the wild comes out in winter," and few animals look wilder than sea ducks, dressed up in their winter best, all black and white with painted faces. Common eiders (*Somateria mollissima*) are the most conspicuous waterfowl found year-round on the coast, often grouped together in rafts, diving for mussels and bobbing around like corks. Their buoyancy is in part due to their down, which was prized for its loft and insulating qualities, and was collected from nests on islands off the coast of Maine in the past. Today, Maine supports the only major eider breeding population in the lower forty-eight states. Commonly weighing five pounds or more, they are the largest ducks native to North America. The males are white on top and black below, with large sloping bills and black lines on their faces. The females are a less distinctive mottled brown.

January 28

Another winter resident of the Gulf is the harlequin duck (*Histrionicus histrionicus*), which can be seen in large numbers on ice-free ocean waters around Isle au Haut, from Vinalhaven to Swans Island, Maine. Harlequin populations have been recovering since hunting for harlequin ducks was outlawed in 1990. They will stay around until sometime in March.

Harlequin Ducks

Long-Tailed Duck

January 29

Oldsquaws, now known as long-tailed ducks, are mostly white with long tail feathers. In addition to the *ow-owdle-owing* call, the long-tailed duck (*Clangula hyemalis*) also makes clucking and growling noises. In winter, these diving ducks feed mainly on mollusks, shrimp, and crabs. At other times of the year they also eat roots, buds, seeds, and insects. Instead of paddling with its webbed feet like other ducks, an oldsquaw propels itself deep underwater with folded wings.

January 30

Common mergansers (*Mergus merganser*) are large diving ducks with long, thin, dark-orange bills. They usually live along large lakes and rivers, but travel to ice-free tidal waters in winter, sometimes in large groups. The male has white sides and a shiny green-black head. The female is gray with a rusty-brown head. Mergansers dive beneath the water surface for small fish, which are sometimes stolen by hungry gulls waiting nearby. Mergansers attempting to escape need a long stretch of water in order to take off, since their wings are small relative to their bodies. They drag across the surface as they try to get aloft. Once airborne, however, the common merganser is an exceptionally rapid flyer.

ONE AFTERNOON

One afternoon you bundled up scraps of slow winter light,
spiny shards that could light your way, you said,
all the way to Maputo. You were quite the cartographer
then, spreading maps, trailing paper routes, assembling
the threads, the strings, the line
that sews us together into the ones: one world, one need, one fear,
one yellow rain slicker of a man now
slipping across the cracked barrens this new morning
to the dinghy you will again
row into the black of winter ink, looking for that lost light that will
let you pass out of Prospect Harbor and
turn toward Maputo, maybe Shanghai.

Annaliese Jakimides
Bangor, Maine

February

Maps and navigational charts are tools of the sea trades. The first official charts of the Gulf of Maine were the responsibility of the Survey of the Coast. Two hundred years ago, there were no roads, no highways, no extensive rail network. Shipping occurred via rivers and the ocean, which also hosted a large commercial fishing industry and provided the route for foreign trade, correspondence, and travel. Yet despite the importance of marine navigation, few charts were available and shipwrecks were common. Finally, in 1807, President Thomas Jefferson created an agency to provide nautical charts for America's growing ports and busy coastline, the first scientific agency commissioned by the U.S. government.

Surveyors needed to use a common reference system so that maps and charts would align with one another, and they also had to establish known positions on land before they could position survey vessels at sea to measure the water's depth. The early work of the Coast Survey involved scouring the coast and inland regions of New England to establish these reference points. Vertical reference points, or benchmarks, for elevation were placed on the coast, relative to sea level. Only after benchmarks and horizontal control points, called triangulation stations, were established did the Coast Survey begin hydrographic surveys, mapping the shoreline and charting the bottom of rivers and harbors.

Today's nautical charts retain many of the same characteristics and coverage as the Coast Survey's earlier editions. The Coast Survey is responsible for our red-right-returning buoy system, as well as many other notable feats, including the discovery of Stellwagen Bank and Nantucket Shoals and the first major study of the Gulf Stream.

February 2

The compass rose, the directional symbol that appears on maps and charts, originated on nautical charts of the 1300s. The points on the "rose" indicated the directions of the four winds: tramon- tana or Boreas (north), levante or Eurus (east), ostro or Notos (south), ponente or Zephyros (west), and the directions in between. Every nautical mapmaker had his own characteristic compass rose, using different colors and varying numbers of directional points. Geographic regions and cultures throughout the world have given names to seasonal winds; this time of year we are most familiar with Boreas, the North Wind.

February 3

As scientists continue to explore the ocean's depths, they are finding new features of the seafloor that are inhabited by diverse communities of animals, some of which are only now being discovered. Fifty miles off Mount Desert Island, Maine, in the depths of Jordan Basin, grows an entire forest of sea fans, a type of cold-water coral. Colorful gardens of corals, some as large as six feet, grow in the 300-foot-deep canyons east of Schoodic Point.

Perhaps the greatest marvels of the deep sea are the creatures that inhabit the New England Seamounts, a chain of undersea mountains stretching southeast from the elbow of Cape Cod, 500 miles into the Atlantic. There, out beyond the continental shelf, corals cling to the steep, rocky walls of extinct volcanoes. Among the eight featherlike tentacles of the

Sea Fan

octocorals live other organisms which help attract food for the coral. Brittle stars cling to the upper parts of corals, and worms wiggle among the branches of bamboo corals.

Corals that live in warm, shallow water contain photosynthetic algae that allow them to create food from sunlight. The corals that live in the basins of the Gulf of Maine do not possess these symbiotic algae within their tissues, for in the deep recesses of the Gulf, light is scarce or absent entirely. Instead, the coral must consume food particles that pass through the water. And so sea fans wave in the current, purple umbrellas of *Metallogorgia* undulate above the seafloor, and large, soft-pink *Paragorgia* pulse like tufts of cotton candy in the watery breeze.

These coral gardens can grow nowhere else but on the hard, steep surface of the seamounts. They are oases of color surrounded by a cold dark abyss.

February 4

Find your own world of color within these deep dark depths of winter: visit an aquarium or create your own. The fundamentals of keeping and raising aquatic animals and plants in glass tanks were developed in the nineteenth century, and large public aquarium exhibits became popular. The Boston Aquarial Gardens opened in 1859, predecessor to the New England Aquarium we know today, which opened in 1969.

If you decide to build your own aquarium, think carefully about what you choose to put inside it. The harvesting and (sometimes illegal) trade of wild plants and animals, especially tropical coral-reef fish, threatens the survival of coral reefs around the world. Instead, choose fish that are bred in captivity, or create a native underwater landscape of local species. Be just as careful once you bring living things into your home, as many a non-native species invasion started when someone dumped a fish tank into the local stream, lake, or bay.

February 5

Elsewhere in the deeper waters offshore that surround the seamounts lurks the monkfish, also known as goosefish or angler fish (*Lophius americanus*). The monkfish is not a pretty fish. Always hungry, he rests his oversized head on the bottom of the ocean and dangles a fleshy, modified spine over his toothy jut-jaw. The monkfish eats whatever unsuspecting prey is attracted by the "bait," including herring, whiting, redfish, squid, American plaice, red hake, winter flounder, and witch flounder. Because most of his body is taken up by his head, and most of his head is taken up by his mouth, the monkfish is also called "allmouth." Slimy chocolate-brown above and whitish underneath, the monkfish moves along the seafloor powered by a strong tail and large armlike pectoral fins. Sometimes the monkfish is scooped up by a trawler or gillnetter looking for other groundfish species, such as haddock and cod. Most of the monkfish goes overboard except for the edible, muscular tail

Monkfish

with a buttery flesh that is known as poor man's lobster. Some fish are kept whole for their livers, which go to Japanese restaurants to be served as ankimo sashimi.

February 6

When speaking of strange creatures of the deep, do not forget the sea monster of myth and legend who roams the North Atlantic: the giant squid (*Architeuthis*). Sperm whales are the only known enemy of the giant squid, and many stories involve both characters fighting it out to the death, with whalers or unsuspecting fishermen caught in the middle. The first documentation of a live giant squid came from Japanese researchers in 2005; the largest squid ever found was 60 feet long. Another large deep-water squid (*Taningia danae*) has bright yellow "photophores" on the ends of arms that flash with light.

Squid are invertebrate mollusks, in the same class as octopus, cuttlefish, and nautilus. They can squirt a cloud of black ink when bothered, and change color to blend in with their surroundings. Their large eyes allow for sharp vision in both light and darkness. But it is their movement that has been the subject of intensive scientific study, providing insight about how the nervous system works in all animals.

The jet-propulsion action created by squirting water out of the tubelike body requires coordinated and almost simultaneous activation of all the muscles in the squid's body. Squid are thus highly maneuverable escape artists, thanks to some of the largest nerve cells found in nature; this giant axon, or bundle of nerves, is studied by neurobiologists at the Marine Biological Laboratory in Woods Hole, Massachusetts. Come April, Woods Hole biologists will join fishermen in shallow waters around Cape Cod, where the long-finned squid (*Loligo pealei*) have moved inshore with schools of butterfish, scup, and whiting. Long-finned squid can grow up to two feet long, and they crush and eat their food with birdlike beaks.

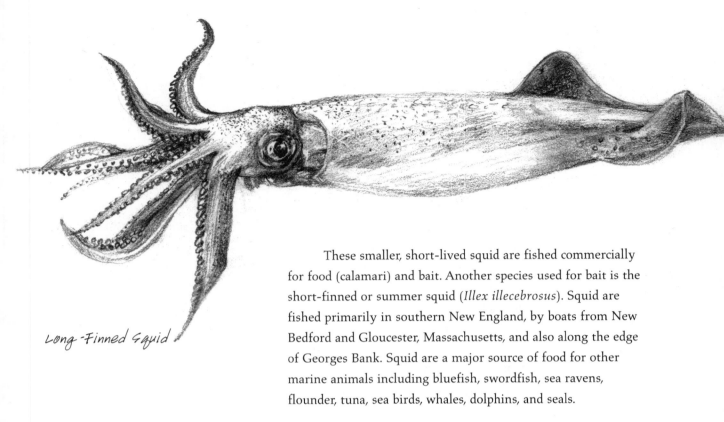

Long-Finned Squid

These smaller, short-lived squid are fished commercially for food (calamari) and bait. Another species used for bait is the short-finned or summer squid (*Illex illecebrosus*). Squid are fished primarily in southern New England, by boats from New Bedford and Gloucester, Massachusetts, and also along the edge of Georges Bank. Squid are a major source of food for other marine animals including bluefish, swordfish, sea ravens, flounder, tuna, sea birds, whales, dolphins, and seals.

February 7

Let us leave the undersea world, and resurface to the wintry one above. January thaw already a faded memory, the world seems to be encased in ice. Ice presents a hard metaphor: it is three times stronger than granite and yet it floats upon the sea. Clear, solid "black ice" is free of air bubbles, a result of slow, gradual freezing. Trapped air bubbles make ice look white, and also weaken it. Water expands as it freezes, but if temperatures get low enough, ice will finally contract with a boom and a loud crack.

On coastal rivers, the ice moves up and down with the tide, breaking into plates and piling up on shore, smashing and crashing, the pieces jostling for position atop one another, sinking then floating, like melting glaciers and calving icebergs. Ice shelves reach over the banks and scrape against tree trunks, leaving behind scars that will still be visible come summer, a reminder of how extensive and powerful winter can be.

February 8

Rafts of ice may become stranded on salt marshes during high tides and, if left for the season, they will melt and leave behind a stain of mud and stunted plant growth. The writer Henry Beston was an observer of winter's toll on Cape Cod marshes: "The great marsh was another desolation on that same overcast and icy day. Salt ice had formed in wide rims along the edges of the great level islands, the shallower channels had frozen over, and the deeper ones were strewn with ice cakes sailing and turning about in the currents of the tides. The scene had taken on a certain winter unity, for the ice had bound the channels and the islands together in one wide and wintry plain."

Author Harry Thurston believes that the scouring action of ice is part of the natural cycle of things: "The ice that has ridden up on the marsh, settling there for winter, has sheared off the plant tops and, like natural grist stones, has ground the bases of the marsh grasses into meal. As the ice backs out to the sea, it takes with it some of this pulverized plant material, and what remains behind is flushed out by the large spring tides.... One way or another, the great store of energy produced by the tidally nourished plants the year before is given back to the sea, where it is entrained and exchanged in a complex marine food web."

February 9

Ice may cause the edges of a marsh to slump and erode into the sea, but such is the fate of any northern landscape that dares to establish itself in the path of winter storms. Ice rafts and ice scour move sediment around the marsh environment, eroding tidal creeks and pannes (shallow depressions on the marsh surface) and bringing new earth-building material to landward areas of marsh that are beyond the reach of all but the highest tide. This addition of sediment may be important to the survival of some marshes, such as those behind barrier beaches, since marshes need new inputs of sediment in order to keep pace with sea-level rise. Without ice and the protection and sediment-delivery services it provides, northern salt marshes are more vulnerable to winter storm surge and flooding.

When ice scrapes the marsh surface clean before each growing season, plants and animals that need somewhat permanent surfaces cannot survive. Only fast-growing, early reproducing species like marsh grass can persist in such a dynamic environment. By winter's end, the marsh may look tattered and damaged, a reflection of our own cathartic feelings: we are beaten down by winter, but will be stronger for it in the end, and like the marsh we will recover come spring.

February 10
With a tidal range of nearly 50 feet, the Bay of Fundy has the highest tides in the world. The Bay of Fundy separates the Canadian provinces of New Brunswick and Nova Scotia. These two land masses constrict flow as the tide surges into the bay, and the water has nowhere to go but up. In addition, because the tide takes about twelve hours to reach the end of the bay—the same amount of time between high and low tide—water level changes are amplified, like water sloshing in a great bathtub. The tide rushes in behind a "bore," a fast wave that forces rivers to flow backwards and brings marine nutrients into the estuary. Twice a day, vast areas of the seafloor are uncovered, revealing large sand bars, mud flats, and even ancient forests drowned by the rise of the sea. Each day, the tides move a volume of water out of the bay that is greater than the combined discharge of all the world's rivers. This tremendous tidal action mixes the water, stirring up nutrients and sediment and making the bay a highly productive ecosystem that attracts thousands of shorebirds and whales, including the endangered North Atlantic right whale.

February 11

Tides are the result of physical forces between the earth, moon, and sun. We are held to the ground by gravity from the earth's core, but the sun and moon also pull at the earth and tug at the ocean. The gravitational force of the moon pulls at the ocean as the earth rotates, so water tends to pile up on the part of Earth that is directly beneath the moon, creating high tide. When the moon is in line with both the sun and the earth, as during a full or new moon, the gravitational attractions of the moon and sun reinforce each other, creating higher-than-average high tides and lower low tides ("spring" tides). During first- and third-quarter moons, when the moon is at right angles to the sun, there is not as great a difference between high and low tide. Such tides of diminished range are called neap tides, from a Greek word meaning "scanty." The tide ebbs and flows twice each day, usually with two high and two low tides in a twenty-four-hour period. Because of the moon's rotation, the times of high and low tides shift later from one day to the next.

February 12

In the open ocean, the actual rise of the tide is only one to a few feet. Only when the tidal waves move into shallow water, against land masses and into confining channels (as in the Bay of Fundy), can one detect noticeable variations in the height of sea level. Other factors that influence the timing and range of tides include the depth of the water, features on the ocean floor, the shape of the coastline, and weather patterns.

The National Ocean Service, a component of the National Oceanic and Atmospheric Administration of the U.S. Department of Commerce, maintains a network of approximately 140 tide gauges along the coasts of the U.S., including six in the Gulf of Maine, in order to predict times and heights of high and low water. The highest tide ever recorded at Portland was 14.17 feet, 4 feet above average, during the blizzard of February 1978.

February 13

When morning arrives on the heels of a really cold night, the rays of the rising sun may be screened by smoke hovering above the ice. The "smoke" is water vapor: when warm sun hits cold ice, the solid water goes directly to its vapor form without passing through the liquid phase, a process called sublimation. The evaporating water takes heat from the ocean with it into the atmosphere, only to later release it over some other part of the globe. In an unseen exchange of energy, our frozen winter becomes someone else's summer thunderstorm.

Sublime is also the word we use to describe something that is lofty, grand, or higher in place or thought, something raised to a higher purity. Henry Wadsworth Longfellow wrote that the lives of great men remind each of us that we, too, can make our lives sublime, and when we depart this earth, like smoke leaving a frozen sea, we leave behind us "footprints on the sands of time." Let the river mouths sealed shut by great sheets of smoking ice inspire us to greatness, to the sublime.

February 14

The enormity of the ocean leads us to use the word itself to describe a very large or unlimited space or quantity, as in an ocean of possibility, an ocean of love. For some, love of the ocean trumps all others.

There is pleasure in the pathless woods,
*   there is rapture in the lonely shore,*
*   there is society where none intrudes,*
* by the deep sea, and music in its roar:*
*   I love not man the less, but Nature more....*
—Lord Byron

February 15

In the late 1800s, the armored cruising battleship USS *Maine* was sent to Havana, Cuba, to protect American interests during Cuba's revolt against the Spanish government. On the evening of February 15, 1898, the gunpowder magazines on the front of the *Maine* exploded, sinking the ship and killing nearly three-quarters of the crew. Without knowing the cause of the explosion, Americans blamed Spain, and the Spanish-American war began a few months later. *Maine's* wreck was raised in 1912 to clear Havana's harbor and to investigate the cause of the sinking, which remains unproven to this day. The remains were returned to the sea north of Cuba, except for certain pieces that now serve as memorials in Portland and Bangor, Maine.

Harbor Seals

February 16

Harbor seals that have taken up residence along the southern New England coast for the winter begin to move north to Maine and eastern Canada in preparation for the pupping and mating seasons. Harbor seals (*Phoca vitulina*), our most abundant and widespread seals, differ from fur seals and sea lions in their lack of external earlobes and their flippers that cannot be turned forward when on land. These characteristics make harbor seals "true," or earless, seals. Several families may group together in small colonies near rocky shores or islands; some colonies remain in the same location for many generations. The female harbor seals that lounge upon the winter rocks today will soon give birth, each producing a single pup (after mating the previous summer). The pups quickly learn to swim, and like all true seals, they will learn to inch along on their bellies when they haul out of water. Once they learn the ropes, seals will go out alone to hunt, seeking shellfish and hake, redfish, and herring. Marine mammal biologists estimate that 100,000 harbor seals breed along the Maine coast today, an increase over the recent past. The increase is attributed largely to the Marine Mammal

Protection Act, which has prohibited hunting and harassing of marine mammals since its passage in 1972.

In *Awanadjo Almanack*, Rob McCall of Blue Hill, Maine, wrote, "If we choose to go into the world of the seal and the sea, we would do well to learn from them—their manners, their knowledge. It is just not the same world as ours. We are guests when we go there. To ignore their animal wisdom may be our ruin, sooner or later."

February 17
The first sardine cannery in America opened in Eastport, Maine, on this day in 1875. Julius Wolff had come to Eastport from New York City, where he worked as an importer of French sardines. But because France was at war with Russia, fish from Europe was expensive and difficult to get. Wolff knew that there was a small smoked-herring industry at the northeastern edge of the country, and when he arrived in Eastport and Lubec he found an abundant supply of fish. He opened the Eagle Preserved Fish Company, and other New York importers soon followed. By the end of the century, seventy-five canneries up and down the Maine coast were packing fish twenty-four hours a day. Production peaked a few years later at 344 million cans of sardines. But there are only so many fish in the sea, and by 1972, fewer than twenty canneries survived, and today there is little left of an industry that once dominated the waterfront. Some fish factories burned and many more were demolished. The Stinson Seafood plant in Prospect Harbor, Maine, is the only remaining sardine cannery in the entire United States.

February 18
The New England herring fishery developed in the late 1800s in response to the emergence of the canning industry. The "sardine" species in our region is the Atlantic herring (*Clupea harengus*), a highly mobile fish of the Atlantic Ocean from

Labrador to Virginia. The Gulf of Maine population is comprised of two "complexes": some fish frequent Jeffrey's Ledge and coastal Maine, and another group schools on Georges Bank. All herring spend the winter in southern New England and move back to their banks and shallow waters in spring. They chase blooms of tiny floating organisms (plankton), and the herring in turn are chased by large fish, seals, whales, seabirds, and humans. So many animals like to eat herring that the fish never get the chance to grow old. Stinson Seafood purchases about 16,000 metric tons of Atlantic herring from fishermen each year; the rest gets used as bait for cod and lobster.

Snow Bunting

February 19

Now, in low-lying fields and empty beaches and dune-side parking lots, large flocks of snow buntings (or "snowflakes"; *Plectrophenax nivalis*) are congregating, pecking at seeds and other fragments of food not buried under snow. More white than the horned larks they sometimes are seen with, the snow buntings may blend in so well with their surroundings that they are only visible when flying, like so many swirling snowflakes. It is rumored that the snow bunting loves to roll around in the snow and burrow into it to keep warm. Soon these members of the sparrow family will change into more striking black and white plumage and move north to the arctic tundra for breeding.

February 20

Razorbills are now returning to their breeding colonies in Maine, three months before egg-laying begins. Razorbills (*Alca torda*) are the rarest member of the Auk family, which includes the extinct great auk, puffins, and guillemots. Auks are similar to penguins in their behavior and ecological role, flying under-water in pursuit of herring, sand lance, and other small fishes, and forming large colonies on isolated islands of rock, cliff, and ledge. Razorbills are short and stout, with a white front and

Razorbill

black head, back, and tail, and white lines on their bill and head. The razorbill is found in arctic and subarctic oceans from Maine to northern Russia. Most of the North Atlantic population nests in Iceland; about 330 pairs nest in the Gulf of Maine. When the young razorbill hatches in June or July, he emerges on bare rock and is cared for by his parents. In two weeks or so, the parents will nudge their sole fledgling off the cliff under the cover of darkness, where his only choice is to flap his wings and fly off to his own hardened granite promontory in the sea.

February 21

The February full moon is the Snow Moon, not so much because more snow falls this month but because snow still defines us at this moment. High-pressure systems that develop over Hudson Bay and move southeast bring with them very cold air that sits above the snow-covered ground and chills the night. February can also be a stormy month, with the jet stream to our south. In February of 1969, a slow-approaching storm brought over 30 inches of snow to some parts of New England. The storm was parked off of Cape Cod for three days, as winds blew in from the ocean carrying large amounts of snow. Though we are still within winter's grasp, temperatures are beginning to rise, reaching a daily high above freezing. Cold comfort during the long night of the Snow Moon.

February 22

Today is the birthday of Edna St. Vincent Millay, who was born in Rockland, Maine, in 1892. Though she later lived in New York City and western Massachusetts, Edna St. Vincent Millay frequently returned to the Maine coast, in person and in thought. She never could shake the draw of the sea, epitomized by the coast of Maine, as in her poem, "Exiled":

> *Searching my heart for its true sorrow,*
> > *This is the thing I find to be:*
> > > *That I am weary of words of people,*
> > > > *Sick of the city, wanting the sea....*

February 23

In her childhood, Edna St. Vincent Millay observed the sea from the Camden Hills, a mountain range on the western shore of Penobscot Bay, Maine. The Camden Hills include the summits of Bald, Battie, and Megunticook, mountains of hard quartzite that was once soft mud at the bottom of a prehistoric ocean. The Camden Hills and mountains of nearby Mount Desert Island formed 500 million years ago, making them older than both the Atlantic Ocean and the Appalachian Mountains. At that time, the land mass we now know as the Maine coast belonged to a different continent and a different part of Earth. Geologists call the process of mountain-building orogeny.

Winter has its own kind of orogeny, as frozen slabs of tide crash into each other, forming ridges and valleys in coastal rivers, melting and sinking as continents of ice and snow cover the landscape. But geology tells us that everything is temporary, even that which seems solid as ice.

February 24

The artist Winslow Homer was born on this day in 1836 in Boston. He started his career as an illustrator and later turned to watercolors. After traveling for several years, he moved to Prout's Neck in Scarborough, Maine, a small teardrop of land surrounded by Saco Bay on one side and the Gulf of Maine on the other. There he painted the seascapes for which he is best known, including Banks Fisherman, Eight Bells, Rum Cay, and Mending the Nets.

February 25

Homer's portrayal of fishermen in stormy weather is no romantic notion. The sea is never empty of some man or woman in search of food, and winter is the peak season for several species of fish, including sea scallops. In winter, scallops are taken from coastal waters by divers outfitted in scuba gear and wetsuits thick enough to insulate against the freezing water. While divers in Maine and New Hampshire are restricted to the chilly months from December to April, fishermen in Massachusetts can dive for scallops any time of year. Dragging for scallops—using a chain-sweep across the ocean bottom—occurs year-round in federal waters, greater than three miles from shore.

The Atlantic sea scallop (*Placopecten magellanicus*), whose range extends from Newfoundland to North Carolina, is our largest scallop, with a round, flat shell that can reach nine inches across. The part of the scallop we eat is the large adductor muscle, which works to open and close the scallop's shell and propel it through the water. But unlike clams, oysters, and other bivalves, scallops cannot hold their shells shut, and therefore cannot survive long out of the water. Consequently, they are shucked onboard the fishing boat and only the adductor muscle is brought to shore in refrigerated containers. The fishing industry cites pros and cons to harvesting scallops by hand, although there is a lack of scientific research on the impact of dragging

Bay Scallop

versus diving. Diving has less impact on the ocean floor community, but many feel that the large, high-quality scallops harvested by divers are those that contribute to spawning output and keep the population healthy.

In shallow bays and harbors in the southern Gulf of Maine are smaller Atlantic bay scallops (*Argopecten irradians*). Bay scallops are found from Cape Cod to New Jersey, but since they were introduced to sea farms in China several decades ago, that country has become the dominant commercial source for these tender shellfish. You can observe the ridged shells of Atlantic bay scallops washed up on the beach, or else lying between stems of eelgrass or on sandy or muddy bottoms in depths up to 60 feet. Along the edge of bay-scallop shells are thirty to forty bright-blue eyes. Each eye has a lens, retina, cornea, and optic nerve, enabling it to see movements and detect predators. Scallops have many natural predators, including lobsters, crabs, and fishes, but their primary predator is the sea star.

February 26

Another predator of scallops is the skate, a relative of the stingray. Skates and rays—called elasmobranchs because of their elastic, cartilage-based skeletons—have multiplied in recent years, which means more pressure on valuable scallop stocks that are also pursued by humans. Scientists have postulated that the increase in skates and rays, and the parallel decline in scallops, may be linked to a loss of sharks, predators at the top of the ocean food chain. Sharks love to eat skates and rays. In the past, sharks would keep the skate populations in check and scallops flourished. Remove the shark, the skates boom and the scallops bust. Such interaction is an illustration of a "trophic cascade," scientists' term for the domino effect: take out one species, and the impact will cascade through the food web to affect even the smallest of organisms (in the current example, think of what happens to all the microscopic bits that scallops filter out of the water).

If our actions cascade (as water flows downhill) to the sea and within the sea, then surely we can find ways to maintain the intricate food-web structures of marine ecosystems, so that all components of our ocean communities can survive. If by protecting the large sharks of the world, we in turn make it possible for scallops to thrive so that we may harvest them and feed our families, our influence will be one of cascading stewardship and balance.

February 27

Henry Wadsworth Longfellow was born in Portland, Maine, on this day in 1807. He was the first American poet to achieve commercial success, and by the time of his death in 1882, he was the most popular poet in the English-speaking world. Through Longfellow, millions of children and adults became comfortable with poetry and acquainted with the emotional power of language. Longfellow wrote of our colonial history, as in

"Evangeline," his account of the British military's violent eviction of Acadian French settlers in Nova Scotia during the French and Indian War. His writing was often of the sea, which influenced Longfellow in his life lived on the coast. He found metaphor in seaweeds and shipwrecks, and lessons in the portraits of seaside villagers. The muse of the sea often comes with a roar of crashing waves, an inspiration as inevitable as the tide, as in "Sound of the Sea":

So comes to us at times, from the unknown
    And inaccessible solitudes of being,
        The rushing of the sea-tides of the soul;
    And inspirations, that we deem our own,
        Are some divine foreshadowing and foreseeing
Of things beyond our reason and control.

February 28
Longfellow once called snow "the poem of the air," the sky's grief "whispered and revealed to wood and field." In the hushed silence of falling snow, the world around us is as still as it will ever be, as if all beings are watching, listening, humbled.

FIRST DAY OF SPRING: FIELD TRIP

Tonight, snow falls. The plow invades our sleep, shoves
through the detritus of our dreams. But today, sun shone

on the first day of spring, as I walked with others up the oozing
dirt road, up the hill, to watch for birds in the barrens.

Blueberry plants crackled underfoot, leaf buds tight beads,
and someone mentioned you can force cuttings to leaf out

in the warmth of your kitchen. The hill's breath
shimmered around us. At field's edge, beech leaves fluttered,

paper flags of the old season, and a yellow birch glowed golden.
We didn't see one bird. No sparrows, no larks, not even a crow,

though the idea of birds hovered behind each rise. We stood around
and pretended to look, but really we were just soaking up the morning,

precious vernal sunlight thawing something inside us.
Though strangers, we talked easily, recalled the winter's snowy owl,

how it had looked like a field stone, a living glacial erratic.
How the spring thaw revealed the debris winter had kept hidden,

the rusted farm tools, broken beer bottles, shotgun shells. How
someone had survived an aneurism, another, hip replacement.

Empty nesting box on the summit's lone tree made us wish
aloud for kestrels, grasshoppers, fresh grass. Stone walls bore

their burdens down the hill and across, and in the distance
thin smoke rose from brush fires, ponds lay white-faced under ice.

Far off, a glimpse of sea. And at last, moving closer, a bird:
a lone turkey vulture, soaring overhead so near we could see

its red, naked head. Happy spring! *we shouted, as the black bird*
tilted and turned, rode the hill's thin heat. Nothing dead down here,

someone added, so sure we were that everything we cared about
had survived the winter, that this world as we knew it was still intact.

Kristen Lindquist
Camden, Maine

March

March 1

Though the first day of spring seems eons away, the calendar tells otherwise. We are ending one season and soon will begin another. The urge to shout, to account for all that has survived the winter, grows stronger, perhaps to match the intensifying winds. And in the trees and islands of the jagged coast, the stirrings of birds are heard by desperate ears. We notice subtle changes in the world around us as we anticipate the coming spring. The smallest shrinkage in ice cover, a patch of bare ground, a drip of sap, branch tips swelling before us.

March delivers both the comfort of the familiar and the exhilaration of surprise, Harry Thurston observed in *A Place Between the Tides*: "There are two distinct kinds of pleasures that derive from being in one place over time and tracking the rounds of the seasons. The first relates to the expected, the ability to predict what will happen at certain times of the year —when the spring and fall migrants will appear and disappear, when the fish will make their spawning runs, when the birds will begin nesting or the first fox kits emerge from their den by the white birches, or even when I might expect to see the first deer cropping marsh grass. Then there is the unexpected: the first and only time you might spy a rare species, or the infrequent visits from a little-seen animal or bird. It is difficult to choose between the two, the satisfaction of one being equal to the excitement of the other."

March 2

Winter storms offer both familiarity and excitement. They arrive around this time every year, yet no two are alike. Northeasters (or nor'easters, depending on which coastal language authority you prefer to follow) spiral out of the mid-latitudes. The ideal breeding grounds for northeasters are coastal areas where a large temperature gradient exists between cold air over land and air over the sea. As a northeaster tracks up the East Coast, the storm intensifies by picking up energy from the relatively warmer waters of the Atlantic. The damaging winds blow from the northeast. The presence of a strong, stable high-pressure center in eastern Canada will block a northeaster from moving very quickly, providing the storm more time to gather strength from the ocean waters, and more time to become destructive. Winds are typically below hurricane force, but can persist for several days to a week, generating large waves and enhanced storm surge.

March 3

Winter storms can carry away sizeable chunks of the shoreline, as the northeasterly wind and currents work together to pile water upon the coast. Beaches erode, bluffs collapse, and marshes slump to the sea. Roughly 17 percent of Maine's shoreline is comprised of bluffs that geologists classify as unstable. Many people are unaware of this hazard—that is, until the presumed solid ground beneath their homes begins to disappear, taking their houses with it. Some choose to rebuild, while others elect to retreat, ceding to the power of the sea. We can build sea walls and jetties, but such structures only make erosion worse by constricting the shoreline's ability to evolve, much as dikes and channels prevent rivers from taking their naturally sinuous course. As beaches disappear because we prevent their formation in a new place, we must spend money and effort to recreate them—over 12 million cubic yards of sand have been added to New England's beaches over the years.

March 4

Although the most noticeable coastal erosion occurs during individual storms or landslide events, the underlying reason for erosion along the coast is sea-level rise. By monitoring sea level over time, geologists can track changes in the shape of the shoreline. The tide gauge in Portland, Maine, shows that sea level has risen at a rate of about two millimeters per year, or over half a foot during the past century.

Sea-level rise is caused by both local and global conditions. Globally, sea level rises as a result of several factors, but mainly because of an increase in ocean volume due to the melting of land-based glaciers and an expansion of ocean water due to warmer temperatures (water expands as it heats up). Projections for the next 100 years predict a two-foot rise in sea level at Portland, in part due to global warming but also because locally the land surface is sinking (New England is still settling down after its postglacial rebound). A few millimeters or even inches of water level increase may not seem like a big deal, but a vertical increase in the level of the ocean translates into a much larger horizontal migration of the coastline landward, especially on gradually sloping sandy beaches. A one-foot vertical rise in sea level along a sand beach could translate into the shoreline moving inland 200 feet or more.

All this talk of sand beaches belies the fact that most of the Gulf of Maine coast is not made of sand, but of stone. The rising sea makes no difference to the stalwart cliffs of Monhegan and Cutler, Maine, or Cape Ann, Massachusetts. Waves will continue to pound against the granite, the erosion too slow for a human generation to notice.

March 5

Most waves are created by wind. Out in the open sea, wind begins to sculpt the surface of the sea into steeply peaked waves (though in winter, ice crystals will smooth the waves by increasing the friction between water particles). As the young waves approach shore, they gather energy and build in height, forming whitecaps. A wave is like spinning wheels stacked on top of each other: as the stack moves toward shore and the water gets shallower, the wheel at the bottom is the first to slow down, and the wave trips over itself, causing the rest of the stack to roll forward, white foam spilling down the front, until the whole pile of rolling water falls on its face.

"If a wave, on coming into the surface zone, rears high as though gathering all its strength for the final act of its life, if the crest forms all along its advancing front and then begins to curl forward, if the whole mass of water plunges suddenly with a booming roar into its trough—then you may take it that these waves are visitors from some very distant part of the ocean, that they have traveled long and far before their final dissolution at your feet." —Rachel Carson

March 6

Winds that accompany the cyclonic storms of winter are also shapers of dunes. For several days during a storm, the winds blow onshore, carrying sand up the beach to the dunes. Immediately after the storm, winds reverse direction and blow from the shore to the sea, and sand can be moved from the dunes to the beach. In this way, erosion of the land indirectly and directly provides the sand and cobble that make up our beaches and dunes. Wind carries grains of sand across the beach in what's known as aeolian transport, after Aeolus, the Greek god of the winds. A strong onshore wind moves sand inland until some obstacle, say a blade of grass or a fence, slows down the wind and forces it to drop its cargo. Grain upon grain, the little mound of sand builds. The grass spreads its roots, sprouting more stems that block more wind. Meanwhile, the roots hold the old sand in place and the pile becomes a dune, a moving wall of sand that both keeps the beach in front of it from disappearing and protects the land behind it from wind and waves. Dune formation depends on the wind's speed and the size and weight of the sand particles. Many other complex principles and factors influence dunes, but in the end it all comes down to individual grains of sand and a force strong enough to move them.

March 7
Tidal height and sea level determine the inland reach of coastal flooding and storm surges that accompany northeasters and hurricanes. According to the National Oceanic and Atmospheric Administration, "storm surge is simply water that is pushed toward the shore by the force of the winds swirling around the storm." Water levels can increase 15 feet or more during a storm, and if a storm coincides with the monthly high or spring tide, flooding can be even worse, threatening East Coast cities and towns, many of which lie less than 10 feet above mean sea level.

March 8
The spray blown from waves during a winter gale is known as spindrift, and the same word is used to describe windblown sand or snow. Spindrift is also a metaphor for those of us who lack roots to any particular street address or job, who travel where the wind takes us. Let this not be a derogatory term, for it takes just as much focus to travel the currents of the world as it does to remain fixed as a rock in the middle of the river.

"There are at least a thousand women poets in America, mostly in California and New England, who walk on beaches and write poems about spindrift, spindrift of the waves, spindrift of the heart. Beware of women poets who write about spindrift. There is a certain peril in this enterprise." —Walker Percy, *The Thanatos Syndrome*

March 9

In the absence of a raging northeasterly storm and associated flying spindrift, listen instead for the black-capped chickadee's song. Maine's state bird is always one of the first to respond to the lengthening, strengthening sunlight. Chickadees (*Poecile atricapillus*) are friendly, curious birds that seem to be always at eye level, tipping their black caps this way and that, trailing their *chick-a-dee-dee*, one of the most complex vocalizations in the animal kingdom. The call can mean hello, be careful, who are you, or here I am. A frequent visitor to backyard bird feeders, chickadees help us through the winter, and remind us that spring is not far away.

March 10

March is the month when owls are most active. At this time of year, if they are not already tending a nest with eggs, both great horned and barred owls are prowling their territories, looking for a mate. The barred owl (*Strix varia*) is a large striped owl with rounded head and big black eyes. He swoops through woods in late afternoon and early morning. He will stare back at you from his perch on a high branch, watching you watch him. After you continue on your way he will descend to the stream bank and wade into the water to catch crayfish. The taller, yellow-eyed great horned owl (*Bubo virginianus*) is a significant predator: he eats crows, skunks, other owls, baby ospreys, and peregrine falcons. Other owls of our northern clime include the eastern screech owl, long-eared owl, northern hawk owl, barn owl, saw-whet owl, and snowy owl.

Snowy Owl

March 11

To some Native American tribes, owls represent wisdom and
helpfulness, and have powers of prophecy, a theme that also
appears in Aesop's fables and in Greek myths and beliefs.
According to Artemidorus, a Greek interpreter of dreams who
lived in the second century, a traveler who dreamed of an owl
would soon be shipwrecked.

The snowy owl appears in stories from the Penobscot
Nation. In one, rivers and streams have dried up, and Snowy
Owl seeks out the source, only to find great beasts (possibly
mammoths?) drinking all the water. Snowy Owl knocks down
trees so the beasts might fall upon the stumps. After the beasts
die, the rivers flow once again.

In winter, if food is scarce or the weather is severe, snowy
owls (*Bubo scandiacus*) will move south in search of sustenance,
finding their way to New England fields, marshes, coasts, farms,
and even airports, any place that reminds them of their wide-
open breeding grounds on the arctic tundra. These "irruptions"

occur every few years. Adult females stay to the north while immature males move furthest south. The snowy owl is a heavy white nomad, hunting during the day from his perch on prominent lookout points, waiting for small rodents and birds. In more than one year he has chosen to spend the winter haunting the summits of Penobscot and Sargent mountains in Acadia National Park, perhaps to keep the giant thirsty beasts away, protecting the streams that run beneath the ice from the mountains to the sea.

March 12

While you are hiking on mountains in search of Snowy Owl, look down in hollows of snow at the bases of tree trunks, where tiny black specks crawl and jump. Snow fleas are not really fleas but members of a group of insects called springtails. They are most apparent as the snow starts to thaw in late winter, when they congregate in large numbers on sunny days to feed on pollen, microscopic algae, and fungi on the surface of the snow.

March 13

More black: the horizontal line along the rocks in the intertidal zone. The line is really densely packed colonies of microscopic blue-green algae, or cyanobacteria (*Calothrix* spp.). This black stain marks the limit of high tide, as *Calothrix* can only tolerate salt water occasionally. During the winter and early spring the band may be very broad, as fewer predators are around to nibble away at the stripe. You can also tell where ice has scoured the rocks clean, as the algae line will be just above the zone of ice cover.

Cyanobacteria have green, yellow, and blue pigments that can make energy from the sun (photosynthesis), a strategy borrowed from the plant world. They make food from hydrogen in the water and carbon dioxide in the air, releasing leftover oxygen into the air for us to breathe. *Calothrix* are coated with a slime that prevents them from getting dehydrated at low tide; this also makes the rocks slippery for tide pool-exploring humans.

Their simple one-cell structure, sometimes lacking even a nucleus, contrasts with the significant and complex roles that bacteria play. Some of the oldest and most widespread living things on earth, bacteria are found in deep-sea vents, volcanoes, and super-salty environments. For most of the planet's history, bacteria were the only form of life. Recently, scientists have increased their estimate of the number of different kinds of bacteria in the ocean to 10 million.

March 14

The black line of cyanobacteria along the rockbound coast is clinging to granite: splotchy, pink, black, and gray Rapakivi granite from Mount Desert Island, or perhaps the gray Mount Waldo granite, which formed six miles beneath the earth's surface. Granite is really crystals of feldspar, quartz, and hornblende that began as molten magma, and formed where tectonic plates crashed into each other 400 million years ago. The magma solidified into rock; if it cooled fast, it formed granite with small crystals; slow-cooling magma formed large crystals. Glacial movement, erosion, and the shifting of continents brought the granite to the surface.

March 15

The first granite commercially quarried in Maine was cut in 1826 from Vinalhaven Island, for construction of a prison in Massachusetts. By 1901, Maine led the nation in the production of granite. At one time, 150 quarries were operating in the state, most of them along the coast, which facilitated shipping the stone via rivers and harbors. Penobscot Bay, Blue Hill, and Mount Desert Island were major quarrying locations, and granite mining continues to this day. Fort Knox in Prospect and the State House in Augusta are built of Maine granite, as are the post offices in Philadelphia, Buffalo, Hartford, and Albany; custom houses in St. Louis, Boston, and Brooklyn; Grant's Tomb and the Cathedral of St. John the Divine in New York; paving stones in New York and Philadelphia; the gatehouse in Central Park; and the curbing in Havana, Cuba.

March 16

Along the southern Gulf of Maine coast, hills are made of less solid stuff. The edge of the Laurentide ice sheet, the most recent glacier to cover our part of Earth, reached about where Cape Cod and the islands sit today. As the glacier retreated, it plastered together piles of unsorted debris: rock, sand, clay. This "glacial till" takes the form of moraines, ridges that mark the edge of the glacier, and drumlins, or low, rounded hills. Drumlins are usually smooth ovals that are aligned with the direction of glacial movement (northwest-southeast). Look for drumlins in Eliot, Maine, Hampton, New Hampshire, and in Massachusetts in Essex (White's Hill) and Hingham (World's End). Drumlins make excellent vantage points for viewing the sea, and because they are at lower elevations, they can be climbed in any season.

March 17

The boulder-strewn hillsides of coastal Maine are reminiscent of Ireland. But this is not a mere coincidence: some of the rocks are actually the same. Once upon a time, all the continents were fused together. At the end of the Triassic age about 200 million years ago, the pieces began to break apart and the Atlantic Ocean as we know it was born. When the great rift opened, it separated North America from Europe, but not completely. Some pieces that were part of North America went with Europe, and some pieces of Europe remained stuck to New England. There are certain rocks that can only be found here and in Ireland, such as the Caladonides, a rock range that runs through the Canadian Maritimes as well as through western Ireland and Scandinavia.

March 18

"Now the world whitens with strong blizzards. The winds fall, the sun is too bright to look at, and the shadows of the straight white birch lie blue and curved along the domed drifts. The outer islands show like cubes of sugar on the blue-black of the bold Atlantic. But the upper bays are white, and the corded wood comes home from the islands on sleds...."

The author of this quote, Robert Peter Tristram Coffin, was born on this day in 1892 in Brunswick, Maine. He grew up in Harpswell on his father's saltwater farm on Great Island. The author of forty books, including *Coast Calendar*, Coffin attended Bowdoin College and later taught there.

March 19

Below the surface of the sea, the earth is still forming, building mountains and carving channels. Pockmark fields are found all over the world's oceans, near river deltas, areas of oil production, continental slopes, and once-glaciated estuaries such as Penobscot Bay. Just offshore from Belfast, Maine, the seabed is belching great bubbles of methane gas, perhaps from the digestion of an ancient swamp, forming thousands of pockmarks in the bottom mud. The cause of the Belfast Bay pockmarks, which include some of the largest in the world, is still under debate, since only some of the craters are associated with actively escaping gas. The prevailing theory is that before sea levels increased after the last glacial retreat, isolated lakes and swamps formed in Penobscot Bay. The sea then rushed in, burying the wetlands. The old trees and terrestrial organisms are gradually decaying beneath the mud, producing gas that escapes with enough energy to stipple the seafloor with pits and craters.

March 20

The spring equinox. The word *equinox* comes from the Latin words for "equal" and "night," signifying the time of year when both day and night are of equal length. The earth's axis is at a right angle to the sun, and both poles receive equal illumination. But more importantly, it signals that real spring is getting closer, even if it does still feel and look like winter in the Gulf of Maine.

March 21

Beneath this month's full Sap Moon (also called Worm Moon or Crow Moon), wood smoke will drift in steady streams from shacks in the mountains and hills to the north and west of the coast, where sap is beginning to run in the veins of thawing sugar maples, and trees are being tapped for the elixir that with repeated boiling will become maple syrup and maple sugar. Freezing nights and warm days will set the sap to overflowing, and icicles of sap will grow from broken twigs. Sap that runs by day will freeze at night, and come morning the southeast trunk will glisten with frozen, sugary drips and shards. The average sugar maple can yield 20 gallons of sap in one spring, an amount that boils down to about two quarts of syrup.

Icicles

March 22

The date of the sap run is part of the subject of phenology, the study of the annual cycles of plants and animals and how they respond to seasonal changes in their environment. To practice phenology, from the Greek word meaning "to appear," is to be an observer, to note the date of the lilac's first bloom, the first robin in the grass, the greening of the marshes as grasses return, the last shelf of ice melting toward the sea. It is to follow close behind the season, turning over each leaf as it unfolds and later falls. And the ocean has its own internal and unseen seasonality, of which we only become aware when the surface boils with schooling herring, or the first blades of kelp strand upon the shore. And yet, by controlling the climate, the temperature of the ocean determines the timing of the seasons in the terrestrial world, so what is going on out there in the deep gray sea is as much a part of spring as sap and birdsong.

March 23

While robins are often thought to herald spring, in New England it is the red-winged blackbird that most signifies the arrival of warmer weather—announced over the marshes with a loud *konk klur reee!* or *oak-a-lee!* Males arrive at the end of February and females in March. Look for them in cattail marshes, the males sporting bright red and yellow shoulder patches. The fact that red-winged blackbirds (*Agelaius phoeniceus*) might be the most abundant birds in North America, or that they are persecuted in agricultural regions for eating grain, must not deter you from rejoicing in their first notes of the year, and glimpsing the first flash of bright red in many moons.

Red-Winged Blackbird

March 24

Snow melts, runs across frozen sheets of river, like glacial waters
draining to the sea. The rivers swell with melting snow, thrust
their armor of ice against the shore, and break loose. Employees
of the National Weather Service's Northeast River Forecast Center
watch the ice, gauge water levels, and weigh the snow, all in an
attempt to predict when the ice will go, how high the rivers will
flood. Snowflakes fall on the mountains, stick together, melt and
refreeze; the snowpack melts from the bottom, slides downhill
into streams and bigger rivers, under and atop the ice. The ice
splinters, spins downstream, pauses; ice upstream keeps moving,
jams. All we can do is watch, and wait for sun, for spring.

March 25

We do have one tool to use against the ice: the Coast Guard
icebreakers. These steel-clad bulls slice their way up the major
coastal rivers like the Kennebec and Penobscot in Maine, breaking ice to ease the spring melt and make room for commercial
shipping activity. Approximately seventeen cutters work New
England's rivers, keeping navigation channels open. They are
smaller versions of cutters that work arctic and Alaskan waters.
The last major Coast Guard ship to have a wooden hull was
the cutter *Androscoggin*, which was built for Maine rivers.

March 26

Robert Frost's birthday. One of our most famous poets, Frost
was born in San Francisco in 1874. He moved to Massachusetts
at the age of eleven, then moved to New Hampshire, and later
spent three years in England before returning.

"Oh I have been too anxious for rivers," wrote Frost,
"To leave it to them to get out of their valleys." So may be the
sentiment this time of year, when we are anxious to see flowing
water again. Perhaps that is why the sight of the Coast Guard
icebreakers is such a happy occasion: they move aside the solid

white to reveal that, yes, the rivers still flow dark and fast. Do not leave it to rivers to get out of their valleys—follow that frozen trail up the mountain and find the source, where water emerges from the granite slope in a burbling trickle. Watch the ice exit the rivers and melt toward the sea, and think of Robert Frost's words: "A world torn loose went by me. Then the rain stopped and the blowing, and the sun came out to dry me."

March 27
Over sixty rivers empty 250 billion gallons of water into the Gulf of Maine each year, the cumulative drainage from 69,115 square miles of Massachusetts, New Hampshire, Maine, Nova Scotia, and New Brunswick. Runoff peaks in early spring because of melting snow and ice, when water enters the Gulf of Maine at a rate of over 2 million gallons *per second*. Working in concert with warmer temperatures in the center of the Gulf, this charge of cold, fresh water triggers the counterclockwise circulation that dominates the Gulf most of the year.

March 28
The rivers also bring nutrients, fueling the growth of plankton, a collective term for tiny floating plants and animals. As the surface of the Gulf warms, but the deep water remains cold, the sea begins to stratify, with a layer of warm water floating on top of heavier, denser cold water. Nutrients are trapped in the warm surface layer where they become available to phytoplankton, microscopic marine algae that make energy from the sun. Like plants, algae store their sunlight-to-sugar machinery within the green pigment chlorophyll. The furious growth of phytoplankton in spring turns the ocean to a verdant sea as the concentration of algae cells—and the amount of chlorophyll—reaches its maximum. The duration of this spring "bloom" varies from year to year, lasting between one and three months.

March 29

The vast numbers of phytoplankton in the ocean consume carbon dioxide and produce more than half of Earth's oxygen supply. In spring, most of the phytoplankton are diatoms, fast-growing, single-celled algae. Over 200 species of diatoms exist in the Gulf of Maine; some form long chains, others colonies. Beneath the microscope, they form a glass menagerie of fans, rods, wheels, discs, and triangles.

Diatoms use silica to produce their delicate, glasslike cell walls. Most of the silica in the ocean is from rivers, and most of the silica in rivers is from erosion of quartz-containing rocks and soils. The diatoms quickly assimilate the silica, and when they die most of the silica dissolves back into the ocean—but some of the diatom shells sink and are buried in the ocean floor. Over thousands of years, the shifts in marine phytoplankton communities have been recorded by the patterns of silicate shells in the sediments. Scientists (paleoecologists) can reconstruct this history by coring sediments and examining the number and types of diatom shells in them. A change in the dominant species of diatoms indicates changes in temperature, light, water chemistry, and nutrient levels over hundreds of years.

March 30

The spring phytoplankton bloom is felt even in the deep sea, where temperature, salinity, and oxygen levels remain constant. The dead and dying plankton eventually sink, and in a month or two the plankton will have traveled 13,000 feet to the ocean bottom, where deep-sea corals wait for this valuable source of food they need for reproduction.

Other phytoplankton are consumed by zooplankton, the microscopic animals that float around in the top layers of the ocean. In spring, the zooplankton mass is dominated by *Calanus finmarchicus*, a bright-red copepod. Though considered microscopic crustaceans, *Calanus* are huge by zooplankton standards:

about three millimeters long, they are visible with the naked eye. They dart and zigzag through the water, propelled by whirring appendages. *Calanus* begin to fill the Gulf in early spring, where they appear as slicks of red beneath the surface and are called "red feed." Rich in lipids and fatty acids, *Calanus* are the major food source for herring, mackerel, sand lance, and right whales in the Gulf of Maine.

Populations of *Calanus* wax and wane from year to year, depending on water temperature and other conditions. In recent years, their abundance has declined in several areas within the Gulf of Maine, perhaps as a result of warmer temperatures, since the species is at the southern edge of its range here. Lower numbers of *Calanus* have been linked to reduced calving rates and changing migration patterns of right whales, and to the disappearance of hundreds of thousands of red-necked phalaropes over the past decade in the Bay of Fundy.

March 31

Some of the animal plankton (zooplankton) are actually newly hatched crabs, starfish, lobsters, and fish (ichthyoplankton), which emerge in time to feed on the phytoplankton bloom. Traditionally, those tiny organisms that can swim on their own (rather than drifting with currents, like phytoplankton, or migrating up and down in response to light, like zooplankton) were called nekton. But as scientists learn more about zooplankton and their complex bodies, the difference between passive and active movers is blurring. Currents and extreme tides distribute the smorgasbord of plankton around the Gulf, providing food for fish, birds, and whales. The sun is climbing ever higher in the sky, winter is losing its icy grip on the rivers, and the spring feeding frenzy has begun.

DUE EAST

They will melt on their way—
islands of ice in easy procession

lured by the off-shore wind,
the bay's silent mouth.

Auspicious, my pastels on the line,
waving their drying arms. Today

I found a new window—to face
the morning's new sun.

Leonore Hildebrandt
Harrington, Maine

April

April Fools' Day. What tricks might the animals of the sea be playing on one another today? Does the female angler fish lurk in the deepest, darkest part of the ocean, fooling her prey using the bioluminescent "lure" attached to her head? Her gray and scaleless skin blends in with the muted deep-sea background, her eyes too small to care what tiny fish or crustacean takes the bait.

Or is it the sea raven (*Hemitripterus americanus*) waiting to ambush his prey beneath the cover of his own body, as described by Henry Bigelow: "The fleshy tabs, simple and branched, on its head; the curiously ragged outline of its first dorsal fin; and the prickly texture of its skin. There is a series of four to eight of these tabs along each side of the lower jaw, three pairs on the top of the snout, and others, variable in number and size, above and in front of the eyes and along the upper jaw. There is also a short but high keel on the top of the snout with a deep hollow behind it, another high ridge above each eye, and a lower one below the eye. These ridges, with about twelve rounded knobs on the crown and two short spines on each cheek, give the head a peculiarly bony appearance." He can inflate his belly with water, puffed up and drifting, looking for unsuspecting clams, worms, and urchins.

The lesson? Beware the light that dangles before you like a star, the inviting garden of gentle fronds, for these are mirages; reality is sharp teeth in a hungry mouth.

Piping Plover

April 2

Even the atmosphere can play tricks on the mind, as when a distant shoreline towers above the horizon, a mirage caused when the air below the line of sight is colder than the air above. During such a temperature inversion, the sun's rays bend down toward the denser, colder air, following the earth's curve, making ghost ships rise from the horizon and crystal cities hover in the sky.

April 3

John Burroughs was born on this day in 1837 in Roxbury, New York. Burroughs was a naturalist and writer who spent much of his time in the Catskill Mountains of the Hudson River Valley. Like Emerson, Whitman, and Thoreau before him, Burroughs influenced American writing about the natural world, including the works of many of our coastal writers. In *Signs and Seasons*, Burroughs wrote that on the beach we emerge into a larger and more primitive out-of-doors. "There before us is aboriginal space, as we stand at the open door of the continent, meeting of earth and sky." The phenomenon of mirage can make the rising sun appear to our eyes before the great star has actually emerged from the horizon. And now, as our part of the globe turns once again to face the sun, we become more aware of that meeting of earth and sky: the horizon, vastness of landscape, time beyond years.

April 4

Piping plovers are beginning to arrive on sandy beaches. The male will first establish his nesting territory, aggressively defending his turf with running and aerial displays. He will attract a mate by dancing, tossing shell fragments at her, and scraping depressions in the sand. Eggs are laid in these shallow depressions, usually somewhere on the upper part of the beach close to the dunes. The eggs will hatch in May or June, and then the beach will be scattered with cottonballs on legs darting to and from the water, with the parents calling them back to the nest with a loud one-note peep!

The piping plover (*Charadrius melodus*) is a federally threatened species. Because they nest on open sandy beaches that are also popular for running, dog-walking, swimming, sand castle-building, dune buggy-riding, and other human activities, piping plover populations have declined. Restoration efforts, including fencing off nesting areas and educating beach visitors about the presence of plovers, are helping to bring these tiny birds back to our shores.

April 5

April is the cruelest month, breeding
    Lilacs out of the dead land, mixing
        Memory and desire, stirring
            Dull roots with spring rain....
—T. S. Eliot, The Waste Land

Budding Lilac

April arrives with force, and life rushes back into the Gulf of Maine, newly circulating and charged for another year of blooming, breeding, bursting existence. Fish return from their wintering grounds offshore or from the south; birds arrive to stay or to fatten up on their way to arctic breeding areas. Movements of desire rooted in evolutionary memory, stirred by rain and light.

April 6
"The whole world is an incubator for incalculable numbers of eggs, each one coded minutely and ready to burst."
—Annie Dillard, *Pilgrim at Tinker Creek*

The mixing currents and upwelling that carry the spring phytoplankton bloom also transport young fishes, crabs, mussels, and worms—transparent larvae swirling about in the upper layers of the ocean, eating the early blooms of diatoms and other algae that now begin to fade. Baby eels like tiny glass willow leaves; sand lance slipping ghostlike through the viscous sea; miniature lobsters smaller than a dime—these are seeds sown with hope, as only a small fraction will survive to adulthood. For example, of the 10,000–80,000 eggs carried by a female lobster, only about one percent (10 to 80 eggs) are estimated to reach adulthood. In contrast, slower-growing and longer-lived animals such as sea turtles, sharks, and whales produce few young, making these species more vulnerable to some threats. There are advantages, of course, to this strategy. Animals that live longer have more chances to mate and reproduce; if they fail, there is always next year. Not so for the shrimp, the eel, or the crab.

April 7
Seabirds like terns, puffins, guillemots, razorbills, petrels, and eider ducks are also long-lived, and the annual nesting season has begun. Birds arrive out of the skies, from over the open sea, for their brief courtship with the land and each other. They choose islands that are treeless and small, offering refuge from forest predators and land-based threats. A century ago, most seabirds in the Gulf of Maine were on the brink of extinction. Ladies wanted feathers for their hats and gentlemen hunted birds and their eggs. Since then, laws have been passed to protect the birds, and restoration efforts have repopulated many nesting

islands. In Maine alone, 294 coastal islands have been designated by the U.S. Fish and Wildlife Service as nationally significant seabird nesting sites. Disturbing seabirds by walking on these islands or paddling too close will make them abandon their nests, potentially losing the offspring within the eggs.

April 8

"When kelp-maned granite sheds its frozen crust, Atlantic puffins pause from their ocean wanderings. From Labrador to Maine and from Greenland and northern Russia to the Brittany coast, these cousins of the extinct great auk march stiffly onto rocky islands, the massive parrotlike beaks of both sexes aglow with impossible shades and sequences of blue, orange, and yellow…. Puffins emerge from the sea with fish draped neatly from their beaks like socks from a clothesline. It seems as if someone with fingers had to have helped with the arrangement, but the bird's raspy tongue holds each fish against spines on its palate so it can open its beak and grab another. In flight, puffins resemble badly thrown footballs; when they hit the water they keep 'flying,' propelled by short, powerful wings to depths of at least 80 feet." —Ted Williams, *Wild Moments*

Puffins (*Fratercula arctica*) are arriving on Eastern Egg Rock and Machias Seal Island in Maine, soon to build nests that will hold just a single egg. The baby puffin will remain in his burrow until he can fly and swim on his own. Puffins like to hang out on the rocks with their buddies, and each likes to be higher than his neighbor. Unlike their cousins the razorbills, some puffins will choose to nest on a different island than the one they were born on, and they spend time "checking out" other islands before they pick one on which to settle down and breed. After five months or so, after the mom and dad have taken turns incubating the egg and the "puffling" is ready to fledge, the birds will leave solid ground to fly, swim, and ride the ocean winds.

April 9

Some adult fishes are moving back into the shallower waters of the Gulf, including cod, dogfish, and cusk. A slow-moving and sedentary member of the cod family, cusk (*Brosme brosme*) is cigar-shaped, with one long dorsal fin from just behind its head to the tail. Spawning usually occurs in late spring and summer, but may be as early as April in the Gulf of Maine. The highest concentration of cusk lives here, preferring to live alone on the hard, rocky ocean floor, eating crab and shrimp. Like their cousin the Atlantic cod, cusk populations in the Gulf of Maine region have declined by nearly 90 percent in the last fifty years, mainly due to fishing pressure.

The Atlantic cod ranges from Baffin Island to Cape Hatteras. In spring they follow schools of fish inshore toward the New England coast. In 1861, schooners landed more cod on the Maine coast between Penobscot Bay and Grand Manan, New Brunswick, than were caught in the entire Gulf of Maine, from Cape Cod to Canada, in 1999. Back then, cod was king, and New England fishermen provided food for their own families, as well as families in Europe and elsewhere.

April 10

Cod and cusk prefer areas of the seafloor that are covered with rocks and boulders; along the Maine inner continental shelf, this hard substrate is the dominant bottom type. Patches of exposed bedrock and boulders are interspersed with muddy basins. Gravel and sand areas are less common. The makeup of the entire Gulf of Maine floor is not as well understood. Places like Stellwagen Bank and Jeffrey's Ledge north of Cape Cod; Georges, Browns, and German banks; and the Bay of Fundy have been mapped, but deeper areas in the middle of the Gulf have not yet been surveyed. Since 2001, American and Canadian scientists have been working on the Gulf of Maine Mapping Initiative, an effort to complete our mental image of the bottom of the Gulf.

April 11

The woodcock (*Scolopax minor*) is a medium-sized, tan, stubby bird with a long bill and large, dark eyes. He is a shorebird that wandered inland and adapted to life in field and wood. April is the best time to find the male, as he has arrived in the north ahead of his female. He hides low, poking the ground for earthworms; perhaps the ground is still covered with snow. Stumble upon him while walking along the edge of an overgrown field and he will explode out of the brush, flustered, flying off with short wings through the dense understory of the nearby forest.

Later, head to an open field bordered by hardwoods at dusk and wait for a chirp and a *peeent*! Then watch as he spirals into the air, higher and higher, 200 to 300 feet high; his wings twitter and finally he descends, chirping and zigzagging back to the ground, hopefully landing next to a female who has been sufficiently impressed with his display. In fall he will be hunted by the sportsman, and before that by the hawk, fox, raccoon, skunk, dog, and cat, but for now he is in his glory, a shorebird wandered into the fields, leaping into the air and singing.

April 12

On this day in 1934, during a late spring storm, staff in the observatory atop Mount Washington recorded a wind gust of 231 miles per hour, a surface wind speed that remains the fastest ever measured anywhere on Earth.

April 13

According to the *Advanced Spotters' Field Guide* from the National Weather Service, wind speeds can be estimated by simply watching the skyline: when the largest branches of trees are in motion, the wind is blowing 25–31 miles per hour. When the entire tree is moving, the wind is blowing up to 38 mph. Above that, twigs begin to break off of trees, and it can be difficult to walk. At 55 mph, the wind is strong enough to topple chimneys, antennas, and small trees. Large trees are uprooted and roofs are torn off above 113 miles per hour. Hopefully, you will be too busy hiding in shelter to watch big trees and rooftops fly by the window.

April 14
If by chance you are in a boat in mid-April on a windless day, you may see the blast created by the breath of a whale: when a whale surfaces, she blows air out of her lungs through one or two holes on top of her head in a visible plume. The blow is visible either because the air sprays water that overlies the blowhole, or because the warm air from inside the whale cools when it gets outside, forming vapor. The shape of a whale blow varies from species to species, and is one way that scientists and whale-watchers tell different whales apart. A humpback whale will breathe for only a few seconds, exhaling at 300 miles per hour and quickly taking in fresh air before diving back underwater as a "nasal plug" seals the blowhole. With each breath, a whale replaces up to 90 percent of her air supply; humans, in contrast, only replace 25 percent.

April 15
Tall, V-shaped blows in the distance are the breaths of North Atlantic right whales, now on their way north from the coastal waters of the southeastern U.S. They spend the summer in the Gulf of Maine, feeding on zooplankton and breeding. Right whales can consume up to 4,000 pounds of copepods (small crustaceans) per day. The North Atlantic right whale (*Eubalaena glacialis*) is an endangered species with an estimated population of 300 individuals. They are considered by some to be "urban" whales, because they like to live within 100 miles of East Coast cities like Washington, D.C., New York , and Boston. This tendency also places them in the path of barges, ships, fishing vessels and their gear, whale-watching boats, and various other human activities.

The National Marine Fisheries Service has said that in order for the North Atlantic right whale population to recover, humans need to have zero impact on the animals. State and federal laws draw a 500-yard buffer zone around the whales, who emerge from the water showing a black head with white patches or else a black, triangular tail. Still, the law cannot keep debris out of the buffer zone, and entanglement with lost fishing nets, line, and other gear is one of the major causes of right whale deaths. Whales must also weave their way through a maze of vertical lines connecting lobster traps on the bottom with buoys on the surface; over half a million lines might fill Gulf of Maine waters at the peak of lobstering season. So lobstermen are experimenting with rope that does not float and other ways of stringing traps, so that both they and the whales can go about their business without harming each other. Ship strikes are the other major threat to right whales, so international shipping lanes have been moved to avoid whale-ship collisions.

April 16

North Atlantic right whales are baleen whales, meaning they filter small zooplankton, especially *Calanus*, out of the water with long combs of hardened protein in their mouths. Other baleen whales in the Gulf are the fin, sei, and humpback whales. Humpback whales live on the sloping sides of banks and ledges of the Gulf of Maine, Georges Bank, and the continental shelf south of Cape Cod. They eat small fish like sand lance and herring. The smaller (about 30 feet) minke whales may come closer to shore.

Sperm whales are the largest of the "toothed" whales, growing up to 60 feet long. They are whales of deeper water. Other toothed whales include the white beluga whale, which may wander south into the Gulf of Maine from the St. Lawrence estuary. Small black pilot whales are now along the continental slope, feeding on the squid that feed on schooling herring and

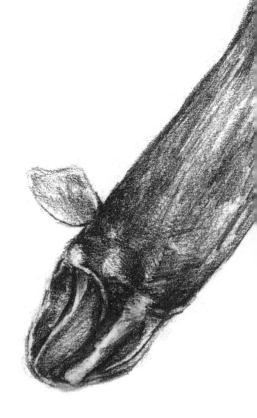

North Atlantic Right Whale

mackerel. Later, the squid will move inshore with the fish and the pilot whales will follow, sometimes forming pods of over 100 individuals.

Dolphins are in the same order as whales (*Cetacea*), and in the Gulf of Maine we have the white-beaked dolphin (they like squid) and white-sided dolphin (who prefer sand lance). By mid-April pods of white-sided dolphins are offshore. Common, bottlenose, and Risso's dolphins live further to our south but may occasionally wander into the Gulf if food is plentiful and the water is warm. Once in a while, usually later in the year, an orca—the "killer whale"—is spotted, chasing after bluefin tuna or other fish. But you are more likely to see the harbor porpoise, a small cetacean that stays close to shore, moving in tune with schools of herring.

April 17
The North Atlantic right whale is so named because it was considered the "right" whale to hunt: upon death, the whale's abundant blubber and rich oil content would cause the carcass to float on the water surface, making the right whale easy to capture and process into the cleanest, brightest-burning lamp oil around. This characteristic also meant that by the year 1800, right whales were already becoming scarce in the Gulf of Maine, and whalers turned their harpoons on humpback and fin whales.

The whaling era in New England lasted until the early 1900s. While the great whaling ports such as Nantucket and New Bedford were south of the Gulf of Maine, cities like Portland and Bucksport, Maine, Portsmouth, New Hampshire, and Gloucester, Massachusetts, all sent whaling ships into the Atlantic. The development of electric power shifted our hunger from whales to coal, and dwindling whale numbers led to international treaties to regulate whaling in the 1930s. The International Whaling Commission was established in 1949, but a ban on commercial whaling (with some exceptions) was not instituted until 1987.

April 18

How do whales navigate? Scientists have theories that whales have tiny particles amid their brain cells that are sensitive to the earth's magnetic field, guiding them north toward the pole. The intensity of the earth's magnetic field fluctuates across the globe, and an animal able to sense these changes (with a substance called biomagnetite) could potentially use them like a map. Such magnetic migration has been documented in birds, and biomagnetite has been found in the eyes of dolphins. Following the wrong magnetic path may be why some whales beach themselves. But all of this is speculation, really. Whales carry wisdom from generations before, ancient memories of ice too thick to breach and songs reaching across great distances and currents where the red feed stains the water like blood.

April 19

Whales communicate with sound. Their musical notes were discovered to be actual "songs" in 1971 by Roger Payne and Scott McVay, who published their findings in the journal *Science*. "Humpback whales produce a series of beautiful and varied sounds for a period of seven to thirty minutes and then repeat the same series with considerable precision," they wrote. "We call such a performance 'singing' and each repeated series of sounds a 'song.'" McVay is active in global conservation and Payne went on to record whales and broadcast their songs for all the world to hear. He founded the Ocean Alliance and continues to sail the world's oceans studying whales.

Whale song has led many a whale-saver to suspect that submarines and other naval equipment that use sonar might interfere with whales' own sonar, in effect by blasting out their eardrums and causing death by internal bleeding. After decades of debate, it seems the whale-savers are winning: in August 2007, a federal court issued an injunction blocking the navy from using sonar during war practice exercises in California waters.

April 20

April's full moon is called the Pink Moon, after the herb moss pink, or wild ground phlox, which is one of the earliest flowers to appear in spring. *Phlox subulata* is uncommon in the Gulf of Maine region, having spread from areas to the south and west and found a tenuous niche along sandy roadsides and cemeteries. This moon is also known as the Seed Moon, Egg Moon, and Fish Moon. This latter name may be more appropriate for our area, because now the salmon, shad, herring, and eels are beginning their upstream movements.

April 21

Today is the birthday of John Muir, one of the twentieth century's leading conservationists. While Muir is best known for his writings on the American West and his efforts to preserve Yosemite and other wilderness areas, he made one visit to the Gulf of Maine watershed in October 1898, when he was sixty years old, six years after he founded the Sierra Club. He was on a tour with the National Forestry Commission through the forests of the Southeast, and he took a side trip to New York, Montreal, Vermont, and Maine. In a letter to his daughter he described Moosehead Lake as "a charming sheet of pure water 40 miles long full of picturesque islands."

Had Muir traveled to the beginning of the Kennebec River at the outlet of Moosehead Lake, and continued for 150 miles through forests and impounded reservoirs and the urban centers of Waterville and Augusta, he would have reached Merrymeeting Bay. Merrymeeting Bay is not really a bay, but more of an inland river delta, a 9,000-acre expanse of tidally influenced but mostly fresh water, the confluence of six rivers, including the Kennebec and Androscoggin. As much as 30 percent of Maine's surface waters enter the Gulf of Maine via Merrymeeting Bay, which at low tide drains through the narrow "Chops" into the lower Kennebec River and the ocean. The tidal mixing in the semienclosed delta creates extensive areas of mud flats, sandbars, and marshes of wild rice and pickerelweed, attracting great numbers of migratory waterfowl and other wildlife.

April 22

In late April the earth will cross the dusty trail of Comet Thatcher, and particles no bigger than a grain of sand will shoot through the sky at over 100,000 miles an hour, disintegrating into light as they enter Earth's atmosphere. This is the Lyrid meteor shower, so named because it seems to stream from the bright star Vega in the constellation Lyra. It is the oldest meteor shower recorded by humans, observed 2,687 years ago by a Chinese man who wrote of stars falling like rain.

April 23

The constellation Lyra is supposed to represent the lyre, a U-shaped harp that was used by ancient Greeks to accompany storytelling and songs. The lyre was the instrument played by one of the sirens, maidens of the sea who lured the wanderlust mariner with their songs, persuading him to stay and thus condemning him to death at sea. The siren's song is a metaphor for that thing which we desire but will only cause us harm… their sad music and watery isolation a reminder that no matter how we love the sea and wish to stay, we are creatures of the land, and must always return to the place of rock and rivers, soil and sand.

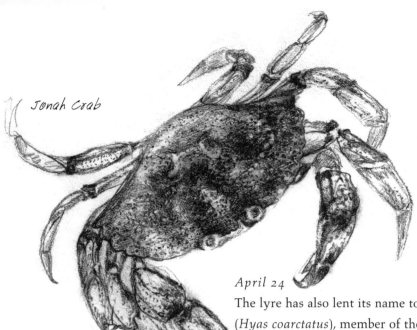

Jonah Crab

April 24

The lyre has also lent its name to the similarly-shaped lyre crab (*Hyas coarctatus*), member of the spider crab family. Lyre crabs are slow movers, and their carapaces become fuzzy with algae, sponges, and hydroids, offering the camouflage that is their best defense. The lyre crab is caught incidentally in fishing nets and drags. Commercially targeted crab species in the Gulf are rock crabs (*Cancer irroratus*) and Jonah crabs (*Cancer borealis*). These have the boxy shape and sharp claws of true crabs. The crab voted most-likely-to-be-seen is the green crab, which is a European transplant that is not quite as meaty or as tasty. The green crab itself is being replaced by another more recent new-comer, the Asian shore crab, which is considered an invasive species. A native of the Pacific from southern Russia to Hong Kong, the Asian shore crab was first spotted on U.S. shores in 1988. Since then, it has made its way north to Maine and south to the Carolinas.

April 25

"In the spring the sea is filled with migrating fishes, some of them bound for the mouths of great rivers, which they will ascend to deposit their spawn.... For months or years these fish have known only the vast spaces of the ocean. Now the spring sea and the maturing of their own bodies lead them back to the rivers of their birth." —Rachel Carson, *The Sea Around Us*

Eleven species of fish leave the cover of the ocean to find their way back to freshwater rivers where they were born in order to spawn (making them "anadromous"): rainbow smelt are the first to arrive and spawn in the spring, followed by Atlantic salmon, alewife, blueback herring, American shad, sea lamprey, and shortnose and Atlantic sturgeon. Sea-run brook trout, striped bass, and tomcod wait until fall to come upriver.

Like other sea-run fishes, Atlantic salmon (*Salmo salar*) once inhabited Gulf of Maine rivers from the Merrimack to Nova Scotia. Their populations have dwindled and today the species is sustained by an extensive restoration and hatchery effort. The reasons for this decline are many and include commercial and recreational fishing, dam-building, water pollution, and warmer temperatures.

Atlantic salmon eggs are laid in shallow depressions called "redds" in gravel streambeds, and hatch in April. Young salmon stay in fresh water (and are known as "fry" and "parr" during these stages) for one to several years, until they grow large enough to migrate in the spring. As the days get longer and warmer, the fish, now approaching six inches in length, undergo internal and external changes as they prepare to enter salt water. They lose their parr stripes and take on the silvery shine of a schooling fish. The cells in their gills undergo chemical changes so they can tolerate salt water, a process controlled by hormones. The young sea-ready salmon are now called smolts, and they begin the hazardous migration downstream in late April to early May, depending on their size and the light and temperature conditions in the water. They take their time swimming through the freshwater portion of the river, resting during the day and moving at night. When they hit salt water, they increase speed (up to 25 miles per hour) and travel day and night, staying near the surface.

Only about half of the smolts make it out to the Gulf of Maine and beyond. After that, most of their time in the ocean is a "black box." Ocean predators include tuna, cod, bluefish, seals, and sea lamprey. Adult salmon spend one, two, or more years at sea before heading home to spawn. Some early fish may be arriving now, but peak migration does not occur until June and July. Spawning occurs in October and November in moving water over coarse gravel or rubble. Unlike their Pacific cousins, Atlantic salmon do not die after spawning, and can return year after year to reproduce.

Glass Eel

April 26

One species does the opposite (making it "catadromous"): the American eel (*Anguilla rostrata*) lives most of its life in lakes and rivers but migrates to the ocean to spawn. Tiny transparent juveniles are born in the Sargasso Sea and drift 3,000 miles north, carried by the Gulf Stream toward the Gulf of Maine. As they approach the continental shelf, the larvae transform into tiny transparent eels called "glass eels." As they leave the open ocean to enter estuaries in spring, they grow into six-inch-long, greenish-brown "elvers." Glass eels and elvers are trapped by fishermen with funnel-shaped fyke nets. Elvers are ultimately sold to Asia, where they are raised to adults and used for food. Elvers that escape predation grow into "yellow eels," and these, too, are fished with nets and traps (or pots). The females continue moving upstream with incoming tides until they get to a lake or large river, where they spend most of their lives.

April 27

Other predators besides humans anticipate
the bounty of the spring fish runs, including
bigger fish, seals, eagles, cormorants, and ospreys.
Ospreys are returning from their wintering grounds
in South America. Large raptors with a brown back
and a white face and front, ospreys (*Pandion haliaetus*)
are easily identified in flight by the distinctive bend
in their wings. The osprey eats fish almost exclusively,
soaring high above the water, then hovering and
plummeting feet-first to snag fish from the water with
his specialized talons, which is why the osprey is also
known as the fish hawk. Ospreys build large nests of
sticks—in trees as well as on structures such as telephone
poles, buildings, channel markers, and platforms. The eggs will
hatch one at a time.

Osprey

April 28

Ominous gangs of cormorants are hanging around dams, piers,
and islands in the coastal rivers, pretending to be drying their
wings while actually looking for fish. Fishermen have never
been fans of these piscivorous (fish-eating) birds, which were
called bad names and driven from New England coastlines in
the 1800s. (In Asia, fishermen took advantage of the cormorant's
skill by putting the bird on a leash to catch fish. This traditional
method of river fishing, known as *ukai* in Japan, is still practiced
by a handful of fishermen.) Cormorants were regularly harassed
and killed until 1972, when the Migratory Bird Treaty Act was
amended to protect them, and populations have gradually
increased. The double-crested cormorant (*Phalacrocorax auritus*)
is the most abundant of six species of cormorants occurring in
North America. The U.S. Fish and Wildlife Service has estimated
the continental population of double-crested cormorants at
about two million birds, with most of these centered around the

Great Lakes and the prairie region of central Canada. Most of the New England population occurs in Maine—about 28,000 pairs. Eggs are laid in mid- to late April, and hatching occurs approximately twenty-five days later. A typical nest has two or three chicks.

April 29
Ravens are being born in the Maine woods and along the coast and islands. A lot of what we know about these incredible birds is from researcher and author Bernd Heinrich, who lives in the mountains of western Maine.

"Birds are driven by their breeding schedule, which is fine-tuned to their food supply. For the local ravens, the growth spurt of the young occurs in the four weeks at the end of April and the beginning of May…. Along the coast of Maine, a most important food for the island-nesting ravens during chick-feeding time is seabirds and their eggs," he writes. Stealers of eider and gull eggs, coastal ravens have also been known to eat mussels.

Ravens figure prominently in story, myth, and native cultures, first as good luck and later as evil. Heinrich puts it this way: "When we were hunters, ravens were revered companions who inspired poets and engendered creation myths. The presence of ravens meant large animals were near. They meant meat and merriment. All that changed when we became settled herders. Ravens soon became a suspected destroyer of lambs, and prophets of doom and gloom. They were relentlessly persecuted because they were associated with death, although not, as it now seems since scientific study, because they caused it."

As with so many animals, we project our own emotions upon the raven, our fear of starving amidst all that is wild. Yet the complex but poorly understood communication among ravens may be trying to tell us something about wildness.

April 30

The mobs of *Calanus* copepods called red feed should not be confused with red tide, the toxic single-celled organism known as *Alexandrium* that now begins to spread along our coast. This bloom of multiplying algae can contaminate shellfish, making clams, mussels, and oysters too dangerous to eat. Red tide is closely monitored by marine biologists and coastal managers, who try to stay ahead of the blushing tide and close waters to shellfish harvesting before anyone gets sick. The location and severity of red tide will vary depending upon the weather, which influences the temperature and direction of the currents. Alexandrium carry a potent chemical called saxitoxin that (rarely) causes paralytic shellfish poisoning in humans. Five to 30 minutes after eating, there is a tingling in the mouth which spreads to the face and neck. Death can occur within hours, and there is no cure.

Red tide, New England's type of harmful algal bloom, does not close beaches like Florida's *Karenia brevis*, or kill fish like North Carolina's *Pfiesteria*. Alexandrium does not even harm the clams, scallops, mussels, and oysters that suck it in with the other plankton they filter from the water. The toxin is flushed from their bodies when the water gets cleaner and they can be safe to eat again within a few weeks. This is poor consolation for the clammers, wormers, and shellfish farmers who lose money every year because of red tide. In 2005, a particularly widespread bloom of *Alexandrium fundyense* cost the Maine, New Hampshire, and Massachusetts seafood industry an estimated $2.7 million *per week* in lost revenues. Nationwide, harmful algal blooms cost about $50 million every year in public health expenses, and impacts on commercial fishing, recreation, and tourism.

While these organisms and their toxins have always been in the ocean, harmful algal blooms have increased around the world in the last few decades. The reasons are myriad and incomplete: pollution is one reason, but it is also true that with better science and monitoring of algae in the ocean, we are detecting more blooms than ever before.

GREEN

Day upon day of rain. Every rivulet and trickle,
every stream comes into its own. Water falls everywhere.

And now we come to green when the wet fields
suck up the sun and grow lush as the pelts of healthy animals.

In ditch and bog, skunk cabbages unfurl. Willows phosphoresce.
Wood frogs talk.

One long day after another spills into each waiting dusk.

Leaves become the size of squirrel ears. Now fish begin to bite.
Everything sprouts on the tip of the tongue.

Elizabeth Tibbetts
Hope, Maine

May

May 1

The first day of May is a ritual celebration of spring in various cultures throughout history. Baskets of flowers hung on doorknobs, ribbons wrapped around a pole, laughter blooming everywhere as spring washes over us with a tide of relief. But what about the other May Day, the *mayday! mayday! mayday!* of a sailor in distress? It is a warped version of the French *m'aider: help me!* A cry for help more likely to be heard across actual waves or radio waves is SOS (. . . — — — . . . in Morse code). SOS was established as an international distress call in 1908 because the letters were easy to transmit across a telegraph wire, not because they stand for specific words.

May 2
"Everything is a verb in May...."
—Harry Thurston, *A Place between the Tides*

Lilacs swell, forsythia persist on tender branches, ground softens, ocean water warms, fish migrate, birds sing, mourning cloak butterflies flutter, the sun climbs, fishermen rev their engines, gardeners sow, and the tide ebbs and flows and ebbs and flows.

May 3

"Dark, cold gray with a high wind…will the spring ever come? How I long for one of those still warm days where you can feel the leaves opening in the sun and the roots stirring below!" wrote May Sarton from her home in York, Maine. Sarton knew that spring can be a frustrating time—either it comes too slow or goes by too fast. The green wave can pass you by in an hour or a day.

Sarton was born on this day in 1912 in Belgium. A prolific nonfiction and fiction writer, poet, and journaler, Sarton lived in Nelson, New Hampshire, for fifteen years before moving to the Maine coast in 1973. Her view of the sea, her home and gardens, and visits with friends and acquaintances formed the backdrop for the thoughts she put to paper for anyone to read. She wrote that spring is always poignant because nothing stays. It must be caught and appreciated when it happens, for soon it will be gone.

Aquarius

May 4

The Eta Aquarid meteor shower occurs in the early morning hours during the first week in May. Pieces of Halley's Comet, ice and rock splintered by the sun, drift across the atmosphere of our orbiting planet, shooting stars that seem to fall from the constellation Aquarius.

Aquarius, bearer of cups and god of rain, appears in the eastern sky after midnight to pour water upon the earth. With rain, the landscape greens, and then the sun begins to warm the mud flats, coaxing clams to the surface.

May 5

Assuming red tide has not stained the local cove, clammers are out digging, hoe and hod in hand. The colder the mud, the deeper they dig, anywhere from 8 to 14 inches down, for the soft-shell clams (*Mya arenaria*) known as steamers because the best way to eat them is steamed and dipped in butter. The clam uses its muscular "foot" to dig down into sediments, and uses other muscles to hold its shell closed. From now through early summer, the females release millions of eggs into the water. The clam's "neck" (the rubbery black thing you hold onto when dipping a steamed clam) is a siphon for pumping in water, which is filtered for phytoplankton.

Soft-Shell Clam

 If you live in Maine and want to go clamming, visit your town office for a license and check to make sure the flats are open; some areas may be closed due to pollution or red tide. Rake carefully to avoid puncturing the fragile shells. A broken clam is a dead clam is an inedible clam.

May 6

From the intertidal zone to sheltered waters below low tide, in hard mud or sand, live hard-shell clams (*Mercenaria mercenaria*). Large ones are called quahogs, medium ones are cherrystones, and the smallest are littlenecks. Hard-shell clams are distributed along the East Coast from the Gulf of St. Lawrence to Florida and into Texas. Mahogany clams, or ocean quahogs (*Arctica islandica*), are similar to quahogs but are found in deeper water, beyond the tide zone. They are slow-growing clams with beautiful, thick shells.

 As the tide begins to drop, hurry to the water to catch the elongated bronzy brown razor or jacknife clams (*Ensis directus*), which quickly retreat into burrows in the sandy mud as the tide recedes. The elusive razors are active clams, swimming about by throwing jets of water out the back end of their shells and moving through the sediment with a long foot. Rumor is you can catch them with salt, which makes them shoot straight out of their holes.

At up to 10 inches across and weighing over a pound, the Atlantic surf clam, or hen clam (*Spisula solidissima*), is the queen of all clams. Surf clams prefer the turbulent waters of the open ocean, burrowing in sand and gravel just beyond where waves break on the beach, from North Carolina to the Gulf of Maine—though they are most common in the mid-Atlantic region. Dig for them on the beach when the moon is full and the tides are at their monthly low.

May 7

Should clams escape the probing rakes and fists of hungry humans, they may still fall prey to a tangle of worms that share the mud flats. In addition to the five species of clam or rag worms in the genus *Nereis,* there are long and bright pink milky ribbon worms. Sharp-jawed crimson bloodworms. Long, thin, elastic threadworms. Fringeworms, covered with hollow gills tinted red by hemoglobin. Segmented bamboo worms, which build tubes from sand grains and burrow head first into the mud. Lugworms, spaghetti worms, spiral tubeworms, acorn worms. Some of these eat clams. It is enough to make you leave the mud flats, squirming.

May 8

If mud with all its shells and worms is not your thing, maybe mussels are a better choice.

Three species of mussels live in the Gulf of Maine: the ribbed mussel, which buries itself in the salt marsh; the big shaggy horse mussel, which forms reefs in the Bay of Fundy; and the blue mussel. Wild blue mussels (*Mytilus edulis*) are harvested commercially from Maine to Long Island. They live in the intertidal zone attached to rocks, piers, pilings, or each other in large beds, and are raked or dragged in winter, before they begin spawning in spring and summer. About 80 percent of blue mussels from Maine are wild-caught, although mussels are also cultured by seeding ropes or rafts with juvenile mussels and tending them while they grow to market size. Farmed mussels are good to eat year-round.

May 9

While standing chest-deep in water sorting through rockweed for hidden mussels, keep an eye out for the slow but shy lump-fish. The lumpfish is lumpy because of the seven bumpy ridges running from snout to tail across his scaleless body. The lump-fish (*Cyclopterus lumpus*) can change color, anywhere from gray to blue to brown to green to red. He hides between rockweed fronds, or loiters about lobster traps on the rocky seafloor. He also can cling to other animals or objects with a round sucker foot on his belly, and thus avoid being carried off by the current. Now through mid-June lumpfish are spawning near shore, leaving nests of eggs in the rockweed. The male guards the eggs until they hatch, fanning them with his tail and hoping they do not get stolen and made into caviar.

May 10

A fish more prized for food than the lowly lumpfish is the halibut, and May is peak season for halibut fishing in Maine as the fish move in to feed. The Atlantic halibut (*Hippoglossus hippoglossus*) is the largest species of flatfish found in the northwest Atlantic Ocean, from Labrador to southern New England. It is also one of the largest fish in the Gulf of Maine; only swordfish, tuna, and some sharks are bigger.

Halibut live a long time (up to fifty years) but are slow to mature, with females not producing eggs until they are five to fifteen years old, which is one reason the halibut is in dire straits. Once abundant, halibut were harvested heavily in the nineteenth and early twentieth centuries and the population has

not recovered, according to the National Marine Fisheries Service. As a result, there is a moratorium on halibut fishing in federal waters, but groundfishermen are allowed to keep one incidentally caught halibut per trip as long as it is longer than three feet. A long-term project that tags and tracks the movement of halibut has shown that about one-third of the tracked fish travel east to Canadian waters, some as far as Newfoundland and the Grand Banks.

May 11

As the trees are in flower and the days alternate between cool rains and strengthening sun, pollen settles to the landscape, forming a yellow scum on quiet waters and washing up on beaches in yellow wrack lines. Blossoms of white are visible on naked branches: the small flowers of the shadbush, which sends forth blooms before the leaves. The shadbush is so named because it flowers around the same time that the shad are running; in the northern Gulf of Maine, the shad run a bit later.

Shadbush (*Amelanchier canadensis*), also known as serviceberry and Juneberry, is a shrub or small tree that tends to grow in clumps. It is most visible this time of year, as the white flowers form a cloudy haze through the forest understory. It grows along the coastal plain from Newfoundland to Mississippi. Dark berries will ripen in June and provide food for birds. The Nantucket shadbush is similar but scarcer; it grows in sunny, dry sandy soils. You might find it in a scrub oak–pitch pine forest or in a rocky clearing with blueberry bushes. The flower petals of the Nantucket shadbush are smaller. When the shadbush blooms, the lilacs cannot be far behind.

May 12

The blooming shadbush signals the spring running of anadromous herrings that are related to shad, the alewife (*Alosa pseudoharengus*) and the blueback herring (*Alosa aestivalis*). Also called sawbellies for the row of serrated scales along their stomachs, alewives range from 6 to 12 inches in length. The females are silvery on their sides; the males look dark gray or blue from above. They begin ascending small streams in the first half of May, and are finished by the end of June; blueback herring follow a few weeks later. Alewives make their way up coastal streams to spawn in a quiet stretch of river or the shallow part of a lake, while blueback herring require swifter and stronger currents for spawning. During their years in the ocean, river herring gain nutrients and protein, which they bring upstream to freshwater streams and lakes far inland, in turn providing sustenance for osprey, cormorants, bald eagles, seals, otters, and, in the past, humans. Those who survive the upstream journey and escape predation will head back out to sea shortly after spawning. Alewife runs used to support a large commercial fishery in Maine, and still support a limited fishery for lobster bait. Though many runs of fish have been blocked by dams, some celebrated runs remain with the help of fish ladders and human hands. In Maine, you can see the herring run in Damariscotta Mills, Orland, and Somes Sound on Mount Desert Island. In New Hampshire, herring return to the Lamprey, Exeter, Cocheco, Oyster, and Winnicut rivers, among others. In Massachusetts, spring runnings occur in Sandwich and else-where on Cape Cod, along the South Shore, and in the Parker, Ipswich, Saugus, and Essex rivers on the North Shore.

"The feast of the season is alewives. For the fattest of the herring have returned, and the land near all the brooks is frosted with their scales." —Robert Peter Tristram Coffin

Alewives

May 13

The coast used to bristle with fish weirs and today a handful of traditional weir fishermen continue to trap river herring in the spring. Native Americans wove sticks in intricate designs at the mouths of rivers to trap migrating fish. Though there are as many weir designs as there are weir fishermen, usually a mesh fenceline directs herring into the weir at night, and come morning the bleary-eyed fisherman has a pen full of fish. He harvests them by the hogshead (63 gallons) and hands them over to lobstermen for bait or to the sardine cannery for packing. Drive downeast to Eastport, Maine, and you can see the telltale stick sculptures of active herring weirs. The crude but carefully arranged sticks are dense as alewife bones and strong enough to withstand the pull of the tide.

Drying fish was another spring task. Fish were spread out on wooden racks called flakes to cure in the sun. Cod and halibut, too, were processed this way, laid out on platforms in flake yards. If it rained, the fish were piled into wheelbarrows and rushed to a shed.

May 14

Should you happen to find yourself in possession of a whole, dead fish, you may want to try *gyotaku*, or Japanese fish printing. Invented by Japanese fishermen to record memorable catches, gyotaku is believed to have originated in the nineteenth century. Clean your fish of all blood, mucus, dirt, etc., and let it dry. Prop up its fins and spread its tail and brush ink or paint across it (except the eye). Lay a piece of paper (rice paper if you want to be authentic) over it, and gently press or rub to capture all the details of the fish. An alewife, which is slightly rounded, may not be the best choice for the beginning fish printer; try a flatter fish, like scaup, butterfish, sunfish, or bluegill. You will need to practice to get the right amount of ink and pressure required to get all the details of the fish. Like all art, gyotaku is unique but imprecise.

May 15

Like fishing for printing subjects, stalking the great blue heron (*Ardea herodias*) takes you up tidal creeks and around river bends. You startle the blue-gray bird, and he takes off with a *frawnk!* and a beating of wings, tucking his long neck into an S-curve, like some ancient pterodactyl caught in the wrong epoch. Or you are crouched stock-still on some marshy bank or flat rock, watching the great blue heron as he stands motionless but ready to spear fish and frogs with his long yellow bill. No matter that he is a common bird, for by his greatness he is a remarkable sight, instilling in us something primal and sacred.

Migrating great blue herons arrive in New England as early as the latter part of March, stay around all summer, and migrate south between mid-July and late September. Some birds stay and can be found in winter in coastal areas or where fresh water remains open. Great blue herons, the largest and most widespread herons in North America, usually nest in colonies, building large platforms of sticks and lining their nests with pine needles, moss, reeds, dry grass, or twigs in preparation for breeding. On the coast, they will seek out remote, densely forested islands and nest in the tops of spruce trees; at last count, approximately 25 percent of the entire Atlantic coast population of great blues nested along the Maine coast between Casco Bay and Machias Bay. Wildlife biologists suspect that, as the coast gets developed, the birds may be moving inland where freshwater wetlands are protected and beavers create more habitat. Other herons in our area include the little blue heron, large white great egret, the smaller snowy egret, tricolored heron, green heron, and black- and yellow-crowned night herons. None of these takes the breath away quite like a great blue.

Great Blue Heron

May 16

Farther out in the Gulf, arctic terns are arriving on islands to breed. The arctic tern (*Sterna paradisaea*) vies with the sooty shearwater for the longest migration in the world, flying 20,000 miles every year between the Antarctic and nesting grounds in North America. Terns are like sharp white butterflies, hovering above the ocean and dipping down to catch fish swimming just below the surface. The Gulf of Maine is home to 45 percent of the North American population of arctic terns, and almost all nest on just four islands: Machias Seal Island, Petit Manan, Seal Island, and Matinicus Rock. Least terns, common terns, and roseate terns return near the end of May and establish colonies on sandy beaches, where they begin their courtship rituals. Terns are fierce defenders of their nests, which are mere depressions in the sand that hold two or three spotted eggs. The nests are vulnerable to gulls and other predators. In their fluttering masses, like handfuls of triangular paper shards thrown to the sky, terns also protect the nests of auks and puffins from predators. It is best to view these colonies from afar, or the terns will dive-bomb your head with a piercing cry.

May 17

The coastal islands also welcome Leach's storm petrels, who spend most of their life at sea, dancing across the waves in swirling groups that warn sailors of approaching bad weather. Leach's storm petrel (*Oceanodroma leucorhoa*) is a small relative of the albatross, and they breed on a number of coastal islands in Maine. Petrels lay a single egg in a burrow among the roots of trees. They leave the egg (or chick, once hatched) alone during the day while they catch food at sea, then return to the burrow under the cover of night to avoid hungry gulls. The chick stays in the burrow through the summer, and finally leaves in October.

Wilson's storm petrels are more commonly seen from a boat out at sea as they search the surface of the ocean for food, tapping the water with their legs as they do so, seeming to walk on water. Wilson's storm petrels do not breed in the Gulf of Maine, but visit here during the summer when their antarctic breeding grounds are bound with winter.

May 18
Tiptoeing around the storm-petrel burrows on coastal islands in May will put you smack in the middle of warbler migration, surrounded by seventy-five or more species of colorful song-birds who have spent the winter in the tropics and have returned to nest here, or else are passing through on their way to more northerly breeding grounds. Tennessee warbler, Nashville warbler, northern parula warbler, magnolia warbler, Cape May warbler, black-throated blue warbler, black-throated green warbler, blackpoll warbler, bay-breasted warbler, yellow warbler, yellow-rumped warbler, Canada warbler…identifying all the different warblers can be confusing, especially the species that like to hide among tree branches and bounce their songs off nearby limbs. Better to take a ferry to an isolated island outpost like Monhegan or Matinicus and let the migrants come to you.

May 19
The May full moon is the Flower Moon, Corn-planting Moon, or Milk Moon. Native plants flowering on the coast about now include shadbush, bearberry, beach plum, and beach heath. Up in the hills bloom trout lily, mayflower, trillium, columbine, and lady-slipper. The soil may not be warm enough to plant corn, but tender shoots of grass are turning the fields electric green, ready for grazing by sheep, goats, and cows.

May 20

Birthday of Elisabeth Ogilvie, who was born in 1917 in Boston, vacationed on Criehaven Island in Maine, and later moved to nearby Gay's Island off Cushing. She is the author of forty-six books, many of which are set in Maine. In her autobiography, *My World Is an Island*, Ogilvie writes of how the island she knew as a girl had changed, and had not changed: "Little by little the names are changing. Little by little the habits have changed, the customs, the very spirit. But some things are eternal: the damp glistening beach and the skiffs sliding down early in the morning; the rote of the sea, as close and constant as one's own breathing, to put one to sleep; the field between Hillside and the schoolhouse when it was a sparkling, rippling tapestry of red clover, daisies, and buttercups; the sea pigeons around Ten Pound and the black ram watching from the high cliff above the boat; and the heavenly sweetness of wild strawberries ripened in fog and sunshine on treeless slopes above the sea."

In these times of obsession with change, we might find hope in those places that have not changed: the fields on either side of the road where it narrows from four lanes to two; the salt marshes protected from destruction; the steep slopes where rivers are born; the granite summits of mountains. Go find a place that has not changed, go to the middle of it, and meditate on the landscape of time.

May 21

If you are taking yesterday's advice, you may want to avoid meditating in the woods or shady spot near a fast-running stream or lake outlet where black flies are hatching. Between mud season and summer the black flies swarm. Like many aquatic insects, black flies are sensitive to pollution and their presence indicates good water quality. Black flies are also an important link in the aquatic food chain, providing food to numerous other animals. They stick their heads out into the current, snagging particles of food, filtering bits of leaves and stem and broken insect, converting tiny fragments of carbon into bigger chunks of food for downstream bugs. When ready, the larvae weave a cocoon and hatch into adults, riding an air bubble to the surface, where the females promptly seek blood. Black flies themselves are eaten by birds, bats, and dragonflies. Male black flies may feed on the nectar of lowbush blueberry plants, thereby helping to pollinate the blueberries, which in turn are eaten by black bears.

May 22
Black bears are now emerging from their winter slumber, hungrily looking for buds and new leaves of trees and shrubs, and scrounging for nuts leftover from last fall. The American black bear (*Ursus americanus*) once ranged throughout the forests of North America. Deforestation and hunting greatly reduced their numbers and distribution, and while the species is rebounding in many parts of the East, coastal populations remain isolated because the forested habitat they need has been fragmented and erased. But black bears do live on the coast; they are strong swimmers, and have been observed swimming over a mile to reach offshore islands.

Black Bear

May 23

Black bears will have to wait a few more weeks for any berries; too bad they cannot eat the sea gooseberry. The clear, gelatinous sea gooseberry is really a type of comb jelly, which is a ctenophore, not a jellyfish. The sea gooseberry, *Pleurobrachia pileus*, also known as sea walnut or cat's eye, has a roundish body about three-quarters of an inch in diameter. Along its clear body are eight evenly spaced rows of tiny iridescent cilia that look like combs. The cilia vibrate, propelling the gooseberry forward. Ctenophores do not sting. Instead, the carnivorous sea gooseberry hangs in the water with its mouth pointing upwards and snares zooplankton with long, sticky tentacles, then spins to bring the food to its mouth. These comb jellies are found near the ocean's surface, staying in shallow water until well into May, after which they spread offshore.

May 24

The sea gooseberry is unique among ctenophores in that it is not bioluminescent. Bioluminescence is living light: in the presence of oxygen, such as when the water is stirred by currents or a wave crashes on the beach, luciferin, a chemical, mixes with luciferase, an enzyme inside the animal's body. Energy is released in the form of light; to our eyes, it is a green glow as if the waves are on fire, a silver wake behind a boat at night.

Ctenophores and other organisms like dinoflagellates, bacteria, and zooplankton illuminate the deep sea beyond the reach of the sun's bright fingers. Throughout the day they drift upward toward the daylight, and by nightfall they are at the surface, waiting for the slightest movement to trigger an explosion of light.

The more scientists discover about bioluminescence, the more magical and incredible it seems. Some bioluminescent animals have personal dimmer switches, and adjust the intensity of their light to match the light from above, preventing a silhouette that might be visible to predators down below. Light-producing bacteria turn entire seas to a milky blue. Squid change color like flashing bulbs, first blue then green.

To see this other kind of light, you must go to the sea at night and walk along the wet sand, watching where the waves recede. Or go out in a boat and dip your paddle into the waves, stir, and all the world will be illuminated.

May 25
"The long slender bars of cloud float like fishes in the sea of crimson light. From the earth, as a shore, I look out into that silent sea." —Ralph Waldo Emerson

Ralph Waldo Emerson was born in Boston, Massachusetts, on this day in 1803. Emerson went to Harvard and became a Unitarian minister, but he left the church because it did not match with his philosophy that became known as transcendentalism. Emerson wrote that humans are part of nature, not separate or above it, and that we are intrinsically good. Nature takes on our mood ("Nature always wears the color of the spirit"). If this spring is cold and gray and you yearn for something young and new, you need only to go outside and find it. If the sun shines but not within yourself, you will be resistant to the beauty that surrounds you. Emerson urges us to look to that horizon, the line where sky meets sea and clouds mirror fish: "We are never tired, so long as we can see far enough." The distance behind us is memory, the space before us, hope.

May 26

Why is the sea blue? The color of the sea is a result of light absorption, light scattering, and reflection of the sky. As sunlight hits water molecules, the light is scattered, and the shorter the wavelength, the more scattering occurs. Shorter blue wavelengths are scattered the most, which makes water appear blue. The same effect makes the sky blue. However, particles and dissolved material in the water will intercept sunlight and selectively absorb and reflect different wavelengths, which can overcome the blue of scattered light—algae in the water will give it a green tinge, stirred up sediment and sand will make it a murky brown. The clearer and deeper the water, the bluer it appears.

May 27

"Like the sea itself, the shore fascinates us who return to it, the place of our dim ancestral beginnings. In the recurrent rhythms of tides and surf and in the varied life of the tide lines there is the obvious attraction of movement and change and beauty. There is also, I am convinced, a deeper fascination born of inner meaning and significance."
—Rachel Carson, *The Edge of the Sea*

Rachel Carson, biographer of the sea, was born on this day in 1907. Carson began her career as a biologist, teaching zoology and working for the U.S. Fish and Wildlife Service. The few articles she wrote early on revealed her talent for communicating science. Her first book, *Under the Sea-Wind*, was published in 1941, followed by *The Sea Around Us* in 1951, which stayed on the *New York Times* bestseller list for eighty-one weeks. She left the Service, where she had been promoted to editor in chief, in 1952 to write full time. She owned a cottage in Maine on Southport Island near Boothbay Harbor, where she went for peace and inspiration for her writing, including portions of *The Edge of the Sea*, published in 1955.

Unable to ignore the emerging dangers of the pesticide industry, Carson was compelled to write *Silent Spring*, the book that catapulted her into the spotlight. To this day, debate continues over the relationship between us and our environment, and whether the harm we cause to plants and animals ultimately harms ourselves. *Silent Spring* was published in 1962; Carson died of cancer two years later.

May 28

Like Atlantic salmon, American shad (*Alosa sapidissima*) spend most of their life at sea and in spring they return to East Coast rivers from northern Florida to Labrador. Millions of shad once ascended New England's rivers before their way was blocked by dams. Shad travel inland over 100 miles and spawn at night in shallow water with moderate currents. Eggs are released in the water column and drift downstream before hatching. The young feed on microscopic plants and zooplankton in the water. Their movements are cued by light and other visual stimuli; schooling shad are easily slowed by changes in the river around them.

"Shad normally, and successfully, avoid bright light. They stay deep enough in the ocean. They stay low in the river… move upstream at first light—an optimal time, when muscles are rested. And resolutely they move in the afternoon…. Shad congregate below bridge piers, rapids, riffles, and islands, and fishermen do, too. Even a big boulder is enough to make shad stop, bunch up, and think. They collect in deep pools in the evening, and go up through rapids after dawn," wrote John McPhee in *The Founding Fish,* his book that is all about shad.

May 29

Native to coastal watersheds from Greenland to Florida, the sea lamprey (*Petromyzon marinus*) looks somewhat like an eel, but for its mouth: eleven or twelve rows of teeth arranged in concentric circles like a bull's-eye of razor points. The lamprey uses these teeth to attach to the sides of fish in the ocean and hold on for the ride while rasping away at the fish's side; many fish survive the parasitism but retain visible scars. Because of this nasty feeding habit, the lamprey has an equally nasty reputation. Yet like all of our sea-run fishes, lampreys are vital components of coastal rivers, transporting nutrients between these rivers and the ocean. Lampreys are primitive animals; they have evolved and coexisted with other native fish for thousands of years. After spending several years in the ocean, they will return to the rivers in spring to spawn, using their suctioning mouths to build nests out of rocks on the stream bottom. They will die after spawning; other species of fish will use the lampreys' rock nests to lay their own eggs. The young lampreys will stay in fresh water until they are ready to make their own journey downstream in fall, traveling up to 200 miles as they follow currents to the sea.

May 30

In Damariscotta, Maine (not far from the alewife fishway), oyster shells tumble from the crumbling banks along the Damariscotta River just below Great Salt Bay. The shells are the remains of oysters eaten long ago by Native American ancestors, left in a pile to be buried and preserved for the education of future residents. The oyster middens, as the piles are called, provide us with clues about how our predecessors lived, and what kinds of plants and animals shared this place with them.

The eastern or American oyster (*Crassostrea virginica*) ranges from eastern Canada to the Gulf of Mexico. In New England, they are found in isolated pockets in the upper reaches of midcoast estuaries. Natural populations like the one that supplied shells for the Damariscotta River midden are mostly gone now, but aquaculture businesses keep the market stocked. Farmed oysters in the Gulf of Maine include Pemaquids, Weskeags, Glidden Points, Cape Neddicks, Winterpoints, and Wellfleets. Oysters are named by the place where they are grown, and so their label indicates the characteristics of the water and, in turn, of the oyster. The taste of oysters varies depending on what kind of algae they eat, and the temperature and salinity of the water. In colder regions, oysters filter water more slowly, and so they have more time to rest in their shells and develop the flavor of their home.

May 31
Near the oyster middens is the grave of writer Elizabeth Coatsworth, who was born on this day in 1893 in Buffalo, New York. Coatsworth wrote poems, books for adults, and numerous award-winning books for children. She married fellow writer Henry Beston and the young family spent summers at Chimney Farm in Nobleboro, Maine, from 1932 to the early 1940s. Winters were spent in Hingham and Cape Cod, Massachusetts, until the family moved to Maine permanently.

TIDES

1.

From a distance, an expanse
of brown—closer up, at the edge
of the shore, a green carpet.
How improbable that this surface
with its ribbons of water, its furrows
and shadows, will disappear.

2.

This grassy shore—so changed
with the tide almost in.
I don't know why some grasses
stand and others lie crumpled
like bedding, shoved together quickly.
Is it the flow of water that makes
this thin strip of shore
so solid, so steady, so reassuring?

3.

Afternoon sun enlarges the field
across the cove where yesterday
we watched bobolinks.
The water's surface is shifting
from calm, to forward motion,
to traveling sideways.
A single sailboat steadily
advances along the far shore.
No ducks float, no seagulls,
no leaping fish. For now,
everything is weightless in salt water.

4.

I think of the clams,
imagine their burrowing down
as the water leaves,
remember diving
under the seat
at the movies
when the music
got really scary,
feel my hands cover
my ears, hear
the hollow sound
of the sea—
an empty fullness.

5.

For the ducks, this cove is both land and water.
With high tide, their mud-flat-waddle
gives way to a liquid glide.
Is it like the change from speaking
English to French, where the shape
of the mouth transforms the speaker?
On Lake Chicawakee where I swim
in summer, I walked this winter,
able to go so much further on the thick
ice with its cushion of snow.

6.

The tide is so much farther in
than any other day this summer.
There's just a thin strip of shore.
Water and land are level as if
land and water were not so different.
High tide has passed but the current
carries water forward, with authority,
as if it will keep coming indefinitely.
Yet I know, if I doze off,
I'll wake to an altered scene.
How different to witness
the slow slip to darker and darker blues.

7.

The breeze is up and I'm watching
as more mud is revealed,
as the watery paths narrow.
My brown shoes sit in the sun
ready to walk, awaiting feet.
I stay here long enough to see
water leave, to see the uneven
terrain. There's still some water
in the deepest places.

Ellen Goldsmith
Cushing, Maine

June

June 1

"It is spring, and it is also the north, and we keep our fingers crossed while the season makes up its mind...," so wrote Henry Beston, who was born on this day in Massachusetts in 1888. Beston observed the slow transition between tides and seasons from Chimney Farm, where he wrote *Year on a Northern Farm*. Before moving to Maine, Beston wrote *The Outermost House* while living in an old cottage perched on the outer dunes of Cape Cod. And so he knew the Gulf of Maine at its most violent, crashing into the edge of the continent, consuming sand and cliff in its grip, forming and reforming an impermanent land-scape, and also the gentle side of the sea, where the tide creeps inland, building marshes as it comes and goes. The tide reminds us of forces more powerful than human hands, and words from *Northern Farm*: "If we are to live and have something to live for, let us remember, all of us, that we are the servants as well as the masters of our fields."

June 2

Spring advances north at the average rate of about fifteen miles a day. It ascends mountainsides at the rate of about 100 feet a day, according to Edwin Way Teale, a twentieth-century naturalist who chronicled the progression of the season in *North With the Spring* and was born on this day in 1899. Teale and his wife Nellie reached the coast of Massachusetts, and for a time the

Gulf of Maine watershed, in June. On the tall dunes of lower Cape Cod, Teale heard the birdsong of a northern spring:

"Back of the headland, where it dipped into a tangle of twisted pitch pine trees, we heard at intervals a wild, ecstatic little birdsong. In the distance it faintly resembled the jingling of a bobolink. It was the flight song of a yellowthroat. A number of American birds, such as the pipit, the horned lark, the mourning warbler, the yellow-breasted chat, the woodcock, the ovenbird, and even the upland plover, make flight songs. This is a characteristic of species that nest on or near the ground. In the spring they mount into the air and pour forth the melody of their song."

Teale continued chronicling his travels through the seasons in *Journey Into Summer, Autumn Across America,* and *Wandering Through Winter.*

June 3

The bobolinks Teale thought he heard, and that Ellen Goldsmith recalls watching in her poem that opened this chapter, are now arriving from South America and descending upon hayfields, meadows, and marshes throughout the Northeast. Bobolinks (*Dolichonyx oryzivorus*) were native to the grasslands of the Midwest, and they expanded in range as forests were cleared to make way for farms. Now, as farms make way for buildings and roads, bobolink habitat is in decline. They need low-lying meadows where grasses have been left to seed, and fields that are not mowed until later in the season, after the young bobolinks have hatched and fledged. Bobolinks are small blackbirds, distinguished by the cream-colored patch on the back of the breeding male's head and back, and by the raucous, bubbling song that spills over the shimmering grasses like wind rippling across the surface of a bay.

June 4

By living on the edge and immersing himself in farm life, Henry Beston sought what he called "an elemental life." The word *elemental* means the basic or essential constituent of something; simple, uncomplicated. Another definition, according to Webster's dictionary, is "of, relating to, or resembling a great force of nature." The elements: wind, water, fire, air—the basic parts that make up a whole.

Seawater contains over seventy different elements; the most abundant (in order) include oxygen, hydrogen, chlorine, and sodium (which combine to make salt), magnesium (required by living cells, including for chlorophyll and enzymes), sulfur, calcium (needed for animal shells, skeletons, and coral), potassium, bromine, and carbon.

The ocean is continually exchanging elements with the atmosphere; for example, carbon dioxide in the air is taken up by the ocean (on a time scale of hundreds of years), where it dissolves and reacts with oxygen and hydrogen to produce acid. While the total amount of carbon in the ocean is about fifty times greater than the amount in the atmosphere, and many carbon compounds are needed by marine life, there are signs that the ocean may be absorbing too much. The more CO_2 we pump into the air, the more the ocean acidifies. Some oceanographers are finding evidence that increased ocean acidity is affecting marine life, including corals, crabs, and tiny planktonic snails called pteropods.

Sea Butterfly

June 5

Pteropods are in the same class (Gastropoda) as snails, limpets, abalones, conchs, and whelks. Instead of using a muscular "foot" to drag itself around, the pteropod's foot has transformed into wing-like appendages. The term *pteropod* refers to two kinds of floating mollusks: sea butterflies and sea angels. Sea butterflies are several species of pteropods that have retained a thin shell,

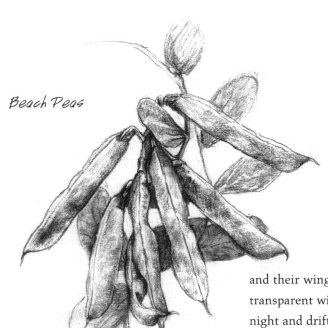

Beach Peas

and their wings are fused together. A sea butterfly "flaps" its transparent wings, floating up toward the surface to feed at night and drifting back down during the day. Ocean acidification dissolves the shells of sea butterflies.

Sea angels (*Clione limacina*) do not have shells, having evolved into free-swimming hunters that look like transparent but beautiful slugs with two separate wings. The sea angel flies slowly through the upper 50 feet of the ocean, accelerating to strike at prey (namely other pteropods) with extended tentacles.

June 6

By late spring the coast is in bloom with more and more wildflowers, including purple flowers entwined with green tendrils and folded, oppositely arranged leaves: the beach pea (*Lathyrus japonicus*). Trailing along dunes and sandy beaches, beach pea will continue to flower throughout the summer, adding a bit of deep color to sun-bleached shores. Stonecrop flowers cling to coastal ledges and cliffs, and seaside irises unfold in pockets of sun on coastal islands. In the meadows and edges of fields and lawns, the purple, pink, and white spires of lupines wash over the land. Though beloved by many, lupines are not native to our region. They are flowers of the West, brought here for their beauty, and now they are a symbol of spring. We do have one kind of native lupine (*Lupinus perennis*), a plant of dry open woods and clearings, which is believed to be extinct in Maine but does grow in New Hampshire and Massachusetts.

Lupines

Beach Plums

June 7

One of the dune plants, the beach plum, is now in flower. A member of the cherry family, beach plum (*Prunus maritima*) is a salt- and sand-tolerant shrub that reaches a maximum height of approximately six feet on the coast. Later, the shrub will bear purple fruit that can be eaten fresh or used to make jelly and preserves; beach plums are also food for wildlife, including grosbeaks, jays, cardinals, raccoons, rabbits, and foxes. As with all members of the genus *Prunus*, the seed at the center of the beach plum is poisonous. The roots of beach plum penetrate deep into the soil, and as the lower parts of the plant get covered by sand they develop adventitious roots. In this way, the beach plum helps to stabilize sand dunes and protect the coast from wind and waves. The beach plum grows from New Brunswick to Maryland, though it is very rare in Maine.

June 8

Low-growing dune plants like beach pea, sea rocket, and sand spurge take advantage of the boundary layer, a narrow space of wind resistance just above the sand. Plant stems like growing dune grass can increase the boundary layer, allowing even more plants to establish. Lie flat on the beach and you will feel this boundary layer, a warm stillness of radiating heat from sand grains. Sit up, and you will feel the breeze on your skin. These plants have

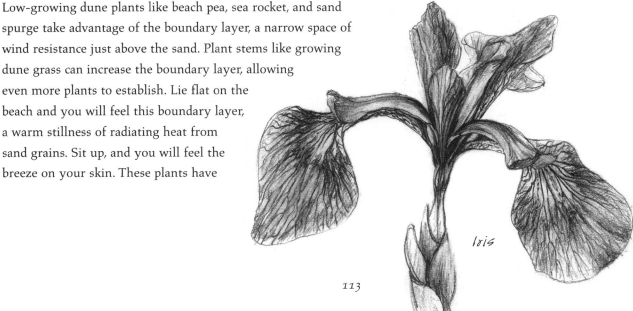

Iris

other adaptations that help them survive exposure to the ocean —thick, fleshy skin that helps retain water, or tiny openings in the leaves that allow salt to escape, or creeping roots to grip the sand and cling to the beach.

June 9
There are boundary layers in water, too, and submersed plants and macroalgae interact with flow. Kelp (*Laminaria longicruris*) is a type of algae also called oarweed because it acts like a paddle in the water. Oarweed has long stipes (stems) attached to a golden-brown blade up to eight feet long. Oarweed grows in dense forests near shore, below low tide in sheltered bays and coves (although it is also found in reversing falls). The blade of sugar kelp (*Laminaria saccharina*) has ruffled edges, and when it washes up on shore and begins to dry it looks whitish, as if sprinkled with powdered sugar. Horsetail or fingered kelp (*Laminaria digitata*) has a wide blade divided into narrow "fingers"; it grows in areas of heavy surf and strong tidal currents. Winged kelp (*Alaria esculenta*) has a midrib running the length of the blade, a strengthening feature which permits growth on outer rocky coasts. The various blade shapes and waving motion of kelp promote exchange of fluid and nutrients.

June 10
Growing in the intertidal zone above the kelps are rockweeds and bladder wrack, other types of macroalgae. One type of rock-weed, also called knotted wrack (*Ascophyllum nodosum*) covers the rocky coast with dark green fronds which begin to fade to golden brown come summer. Rockweed anchors to rocks with a disc-shaped holdfast, and air bladders keep the fronds afloat. After their reproduction phase in April and May, rockweed fronds break off and drift out to sea where they form extensive, free-floating mats. The mats can take up acres of the ocean surface; for two or three months in the summer they form a

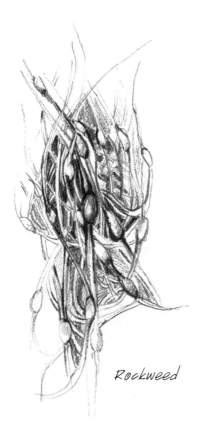
Rockweed

temporary habitat. The rockweed mats eventually return to shore with the tide, where they are broken down into essential nutrients that are washed back into the sea.

In addition to being slippery and dangerous, walking on rockweed can harm or weaken the stalks, making the algae more vulnerable to breaking during storms. A single rockweed can live for decades; counting the air bladders along the main stalk is a quick and easy way to assess its age: the more bladders you count along the longest or fattest stem, the older the rockweed. In general.

Wormweed is a variety of rockweed that grows near the high-tide line, close to salt-marsh grasses. It is yellower than knotted wrack. Bladder wrack (*Fucus* spp.) is seen mixed with rockweed or growing just above or below it. Fucus has Y-shaped, flattened blades containing bladders and a midrib. The reproductive structures are within the swollen tips of the blades.

June 11

"The sea, once it casts its spell, holds one in its net of wonder forever." —Jacques Cousteau

Today is the birthday of Jacques Yves Cousteau, "The Captain," who helped develop the Aqua-Lung (predecessor to scuba gear) in 1943 and traveled the seas in the *Calypso*, sharing the ocean with the world in over one hundred television programs and fifty books. Cousteau put cameras in watertight boxes and dropped them into the sea so that people could see what lived beneath, believing that, like himself, people would love what they saw and protect what they love.

June 12

The sea has cast its spell on you, and you find yourself aging rockweed and sorting through kelp fronds and watching sand grains tumble across the beach. You want to take the sea with you. Find a piece of seaweed that has been freshly deposited on shore or has broken off, rather than picking a living frond. Keep it wetted with salt water, perhaps in a bucket, until you get home. Put a piece of watercolor paper in a shallow tray and fill the tray with fresh water. Add your specimen and, with tweezers, carefully separate the fronds and position them as you like. Slowly, keeping the paper flat, lift it up and out of the tray, keeping the seaweed in position. A few more adjustments with the tweezers and it is ready to press beneath newspapers and heavy books. When it dries, label the seaweed with the species, place found, and date. Frame it well to eliminate exposure to air, which will cause fading and breakage.

June 13

Black sea bass (*Centropristis striata*) have moved close to shore to spawn, sometimes in water only a few feet deep, in southern New England waters. The breeding males sport a pronounced blue hump on their heads. The Gulf of Maine is the northern end of the species' range, which extends to Florida and the Gulf of Mexico. Black sea bass are related to groupers and like to hang around sunken shipwrecks, reefs, piers, and jetties in areas of rocky bottom. They will stay around until the water gets cold in the fall, when they will move offshore along the edge of the continental shelf.

June 14

Tiger swallowtail butterflies arrive beginning about now, their large yellow-and-black wings fluttering across roads and fields. In the southern Gulf of Maine watershed, the species are eastern tiger swallowtails (*Papilio glaucus*); in the north, you are more likely to encounter the smaller Canadian tiger swallowtail (*Papilio arcticus*). Caterpillars are picky about what they eat, and an adult female butterfly will carefully target a plant on which to lay her eggs in order to ensure that her offspring enter the world surrounded by their favorite food. Tiger swallowtail caterpillars gorge on the leaves of aspen, birch, and cherry; adults take flight from now through July. The new leaves are unfurled but still tender—a sign that butterfly season is upon us.

June 15
Amy Clampitt, a poet who spent time on the Maine coast, was born on this day in 1920. Clampitt achieved literary acclaim late in life, but still continued to rent a summer cottage in Corea, Maine. In the introduction to Clampitt's *Collected Poems*, Mary Jo Salter wrote that Maine was "a sort of no-home away from no-home; she treasured her Down East friends, the view of 'Tit Manan lighthouse and the walk to the outer bar, but she took a pointed pleasure in not really belonging to Corea any more than she did to Manhattan or had to Iowa." Here, from her poem "Beach Glass":

The houses
of so many mussels and periwinkles
have been abandoned here, it's hopeless
to know which to salvage. Instead
I keep a lookout for beach glass—
amber of Budweiser, chrysoprase
of Almaden and Gallo, lapis
by way of (no getting around it,
I'm afraid) Phillips'
Milk of Magnesia, with now and then a rare
translucent turquoise or blurred amethyst of no known origin.

June 16
Whispers among beachcombers and jewelry makers say that beach glass is becoming scarce. First, plastic bits far outnumber glass pieces in the ocean, despite anti-dumping laws and a sup- posedly elevated environmental consciousness. The shipwrecks

and sunken treasure chests have given up most of their supply of old broken glass, which has long since washed ashore and been plucked by eagle-eyed sea-glass harvesters. Much of the "beach glass" jewelry today is made from factory-tumbled glass, no more recycled than the glass in a curbside bin. Real beach glass is uneven and pitted, and do not even think about picking it up unless it is completely cloudy and rounded. The impatient beachgoer may be tempted to pick up anything glassy, white or brown or blue or green, but the ocean needs to do its work. Some people have gotten so desperate they have (unsuccessfully) begged fishermen to dump broken glass at sea in the hopes it will wash up on their particular beach. The point of all this is that beach glass was always a special find, and now is even more so.

June 17

In mid-June, periwinkles move into shallow waters for mating. These snails scrape algae from the rocks of the tidal zone, keeping the green scum in check and holding on tight when the tide comes in and out. We have three species of periwinkle, all in varying shades of brown and purple. They are pickled and eaten as "wrinkles." Common periwinkle (*Littorina littorea*) prefers the low to mid-tide zone, rough periwinkle (*Littorina saxatilis*) likes it a bit higher, and smooth periwinkle (*Littorina obtusata*) hides among fronds of rockweed.

Periwinkles are preyed on by moon snails (*Lunatia heros*), which attach themselves to the periwinkle and discharge a mild acid that softens the victim's shell. This allows the moon snail to get at the body inside with its hard, rasping tongue, leaving behind a telltale drill hole in the shell. When the moon snail lays her eggs, she cements them together with sand and slime, forming a flexible "collar" that looks like a piece of pale rubber or broken pottery. In about a month the eggs will hatch and the collar will fall apart. A collar washed up on the beach may turn dry and brittle.

June 18

This month's full moon is the Strawberry Moon, in recognition of the strawberry harvest season. Strawberry fields can be found throughout the Gulf of Maine watershed, and many are pick-your-own, offering nonfarming folks the chance to get outside, feel the summer heat, and enjoy the first fruits of the season. Even better are wild strawberries, which grow prostrate in sunny meadows and tame edges of woods, bearing tiny, tender, cone-shaped berries among thin three-part leaflets. Wild strawberries are only around for a brief window of time before they are eaten by birds and other animals or simply fade on the vine.

June 19

Horseshoe crabs, having spent the last month gorging on mussels, clams, and worms, are moving into shallow bays and estuaries to breed. In late spring, around the time of the full moon, they clamber ashore in great piles, the males clinging to the females waiting for the chance to fertilize hundreds of tiny green eggs laid in the damp sand and mud just beyond the reach of the highest tide.

The horseshoe crab (*Limulus polyphemus*) is not a crab at all but more closely related to scorpions and spiders. A hard, knifelike tail extends from the back of the horseshoe crab, which the crab uses to right itself after being flipped over by waves or curious humans. Horseshoe crabs do not bite or sting. Empty shells on beaches are leftovers from molting, which occurs periodically as the crab grows.

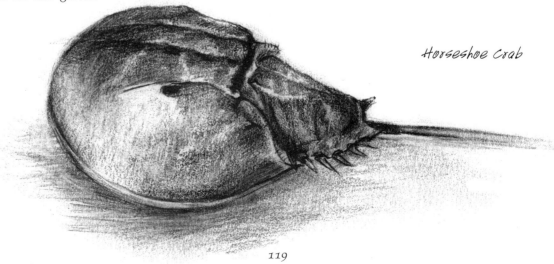

Horseshoe Crab

Horseshoe crabs are prehistoric animals, the descendants of trilobites that lived on the ocean floor over 400 million years ago. They survived what the dinosaurs could not. Continents collided, ice ages came and went, and the horseshoe crabs kept on keepin' on, and they are still here. They must be fairly resistant to whatever nature or technology can throw at them. They also save lives: a protein in their blood is used to test for bacterial toxins during medical operations. Harvesting their blood does not kill horseshoe crabs, but catching them for bait and fertilizer does. Horseshoe crabs range discontinuously along the coast from the Yucatan Peninsula of Mexico to Taunton Bay in Maine, and in some areas such as Delaware Bay their eggs are a primary food for migrating shorebirds like the red knot.

June 20
The blackpoll warbler (*Dendroica striata*) always seems to arrive later than the other songbirds, and for this reason he has been called the harbinger of summer. He straggles in, his long 1,800-mile nonstop journey from South America to the boreal forest almost complete. His song is high-pitched, his black cap and white cheeks puffed with exertion. When you hear his repetitive, squeaking *tsit, tsit, tsit, tsit, tsit, tsit!* summer cannot be far behind.

June 21
The summer solstice. The North Pole is closest to the sun, making today the longest day of the year and a traditional celebratory day in northern regions around the globe. It is also the birthday of artist Rockwell Kent, who lived and painted on Monhegan Island, Maine, for five years beginning in 1905.

June 22

Fireflies begin to light up the summer night like wandering stars. Fireflies are members of the family Lampyridae, which are not really flies at all, but beetles. They like to live near water. Male fireflies (or "lightning bugs") emit a pattern of flashes using bioluminescence, communicating to the flightless females waiting in the grass below. The females flash back and the males drop down toward the beckoning signals. Each species has its own code of flashes, a way to ensure that males and females of the same species find each other for mating.

Once a common sight on summer nights, fireflies seem to be declining around the world but no one knows why. Your best chance to see them is in a wet meadow or woods near a lake, before midnight on a warm, humid night in June or July.

June 23

Not a rare sight is the mosquito. Roughly forty species of mosquitoes make the Northeast their home, but not all of them bite people. Some prefer frogs, snakes, and other cold-blooded animals. Others prey primarily on birds. Only female mosquitoes bite; they need a victim's blood for the development of eggs inside their bodies. Female mosquitoes are voracious insects; they draw up to three times their body weight in blood and can barely fly away to digest their meals. Males feed exclusively on nectar. The insect's distinctive buzz is made by its wings, which move about 1,000 times a second. The female's wings make a higher-pitched tone than the male's, which helps them find mates. Two huge compound eyes cover most of their heads, but mosquitoes find their prey mainly by smell. Carbon dioxide, exhaled in our breath and given off in other body vapors, leads them to humans.

On the coast, salt-marsh mosquitoes (*Aedes cantator, Aedes sollicitans, Aedes taeniorhynchus*) produce many generations per year and fly much longer distances, 20 miles or more, in search of food. These species breed only in saline pools in or near salt marshes. Their populations are linked to the frequency of spring tides. Marshes throughout New England bear the scars of ill-fated attempts at eliminating mosquitoes: straight ditches and blasted holes. Other marshes have been drained or filled in.

June 24
Sweetgrass is coming into bloom in wet meadows, marshes, and shaded stream banks from Labrador to New Jersey and west across the northern tier of the continent. Sweetgrass is named for the vanilla-like fragrance that grows even stronger when the grass has been harvested and dried, as by Native American traditional basketmakers. The grass will continue to flower until August, although harvest peaks in late June and early July. Look for the two-foot-tall grass growing along with other grasses and shrubs; sweetgrass has smooth, upright stems and long, narrow, flat leaves. The flowers are clustered into spikelets on a four-inch flower head. Of course, the best way to identify it is by smell. *Hierochloe odorata* owes its fragrance to coumarin, a natural chemical also found in lavender, licorice, strawberries, apricots, cherries, cinnamon, and sweet clover. Native Americans use sweetgrass ceremonially through burning, and in basketmaking. *Hierochloe* translates from the Greek as "sacred grass," or holy grass. It is the grass that never dies: even when cut, it retains its fragrance and spirit, an apt metaphor for these full days of early summer, when it seems the season will never die.

June 25
Now clear bays and estuaries undulate with *monami,* the synchronized waving motion of underwater sea grasses. Blades of eelgrass (*Zostera marina*) look similar to the wild celery of

Eelgrass

freshwater rivers, or the flat green ribbons of mermaid's hair tangled in the current. Eelgrass and other sea grasses are called "ecosystem engineers" because they create and alter habitat. Beds of eelgrass, growing in isolated patches and in large meadows, provide shelter and nursery grounds for fish and shellfish, as well as food for waterfowl. Baby blue mussels will settle on blades of eelgrass for a few weeks before moving to mussel bars for a permanent home. Eelgrass beds alter habitat by trapping sand and sediment among the stems, helping to stabilize shoreline areas. Sea grasses also help keep bays clean by taking up nutrients from the water around them. Eelgrass is a true grass that flowers underwater, though it is more closely related to lilies than actual grass. The flowers are small and they have no need for insects, as pollination takes place via currents.

Many eelgrass beds along the Maine coast have disappeared, but scientists are still studying whether it is part of a widespread decline or an alternating cycle, as new eelgrass beds have appeared elsewhere.

June 26

Bluefish return from their wintering grounds off south Florida and begin the feeding frenzy that by the end of summer will have consumed over one billion fish in New England waters. Bluefish (*Pomatomus saltatrix*) will eat almost anything they can catch and swallow: butterfish, mackerel—even lobster, which they tear apart with sharp teeth and strong jaws. Bluefish congregate with other bluefish of similar size, forming schools that can cover tens of square miles of ocean. Early in the season they feed offshore on the bottom. Later they are seen harassing other fish near the surface. In *Recreational Fisheries of Coastal New England*, Robert Biagi and Michael Ross write, "Bluefish dash wildly about within schools of prey species, biting, crippling, and killing numerous small fishes, most of which are subsequently eaten. They frequently drive schools of prey species into shallow inshore areas where it is easier to cripple or catch individuals trying to escape. (Infrequently) during particularly frenzied feeding activity, schooling fishes such as menhaden will literally be driven to shore, leaving a number of individuals beached along the wave line." Their aggressive nature makes them popular with recreational fishermen, and in fact most of the quota (catch allowed by the Atlantic States Marine Fisheries Commission) is allocated to the recreational sector. Bluefish are oily, fishy-tasting fish best eaten fresh. Juvenile bluefish, known as snappers, are also fun to catch from bridges over tidal inlets and estuaries. Coat them with breadcrumbs and fry them whole.

June 27
Easily recognized by the seven or eight dark stripes running the length of its silver body, the striped bass is an anadromous schooling fish of the Atlantic coast. A long-lived (up to 40 years) and large (up to 100 pounds) fish, the striped bass (*Morone saxatilis*) was one of the most important recreational and commercial fishes of the Northeast. Millions of pounds of striped bass were caught every year by commercial and recreational fishermen until the mid-1970s when the population started to shrink. In the 1980s, there were so few striped bass that some considered placing them on the endangered species list. Bans on fishing and strict regulations allowed stocks to rebound, and today their range is expanding.

Come spring, they will leave their main spawning grounds of the Chesapeake, Delaware, and Hudson estuaries and move north into shallow bays, rocky shores, coastal rivers, and along the surf line of barrier beaches. New England's only known spawning population of striped bass is in Maine's Kennebec River.

June 28

The favorite food of striped bass are menhaden, or pogies, which are now moving into the Gulf of Maine for the summer. *Brevoortia tyrannus* are small, blue-black fish with silvery sides and deeply forked tails. Menhaden travel in huge schools, feeding on phytoplankton and swimming in circles. They will make the surface of a bay ripple, and will even poke their snouts above the water. Too many menhaden in too shallow a cove will use up all the oxygen in the water, and the fish will suffocate and wash ashore in massive fish kills. Just before death, the fish can be seen swimming very slowly in a disoriented manner just below the surface of the water.

Atlantic menhaden have supported one of the United States' largest fisheries since colonial times. Millions of tons of menhaden were caught for fertilizer, protein, and fish oil, which was used to make soap, linoleum, waterproof fabrics, and paint. Atlantic menhaden will not bite a baited hook, but they are easily caught with nets and are a major target of commercial fishermen for both food and bait.

June 29

Celia Thaxter, who was born on this day in 1835 in Portsmouth, New Hampshire, spent most of her life on the Isles of Shoals, a group of nine small islands around the offshore border of Maine and New Hampshire. She lived on the mainland for only a brief time, and soon fled back to Appledore Island, where she wrote of the contrast in time: "The eternal sound of the sea on every side has a tendency to wear away the edge of human thought and perception; sharp outlines become blurred and softened like a sketch in charcoal; nothing appeals to the mind with the same distinctions as on the mainland, amid the rush and stir of people and things, and the excitements of social life."

June 30

The Isles of Shoals comprise an archipelago, many islands in an expanse of water. It is a word used to describe any group of things that are isolated and separate yet related in some way. Island Institute director Philip Conkling estimates the Maine archipelago at more than 3,000 islands, depending on the tide. He writes in *Islands in Time*, "Out there, between the point where you can take your last dry step and the faint horizon of your mind's eye, lies another world, apart. A world of islands— part sea, part rock; part wild, part subdued; part fish, part man; and with winged birds between. From the tip of Cape Elizabeth or Cape Wash, from Cape Small or Cape Split, from the ends of Schoodic Point or Pemaquid Point, from Newbury Neck or Linekin Neck, from Owl's Head or Schooner Head, you can see them out there like sequins—small and shining objects in the water. Islands. Not just a few islands, but countless multitudes of great and little wave-washed rocks. A lifetime's worth of islands, apart and between."

July

HAIKU

rock shelter
brittle star unfolds
sea water takes in the light

Cheryl Daigle
Old Town, Maine

July

July 1

Where the brittle star unfolds, seawater takes in light and heat from the summer sun. The Gulf of Maine stratifies into layers, with warmer water floating on top of colder, saltier water. Stratification is most pronounced in the deeper areas of the western Gulf. The counterclockwise circulation in the Gulf strengthens in the top layer, and the Eastern Maine Coastal Current intensifies.

Warm, weak southwest winds blow off the land, stirring up the surface of the ocean, and the shattering waves send particles of salt into the air. Water from the humid air, now over the colder ocean, condenses around the salt and is carried toward shore by the sea breeze. Tongues of fog roll off the ocean and creep into harbors. Fog surrounds the tops of coastal mountains and cliffs, lingering into the morning and finally evaporating beneath the beating sun, leaving the salt behind. Fog is a cloud that has formed close to earth. You can feel it on your skin like sweat, tiny crystals blown in from a distant sea.

July 2

Brittle stars and sea stars are members of the Echinoderm family, which includes 40 other species that share certain characteristics, namely spiny skin and five-part body symmetry. With five arms and a calcium carbonate skeleton, brittle stars crawl, wiggle, and row across the seafloor and among corals, scavenging for

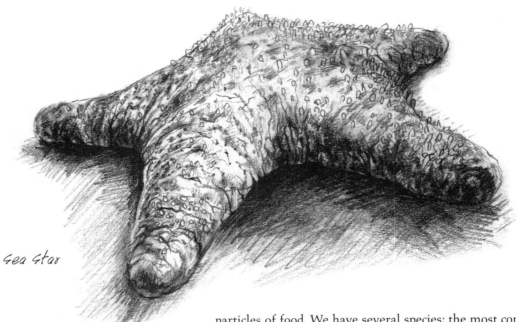

Sea Star

particles of food. We have several species; the most common and easily seen is the daisy brittle star (*Ophiopholis aculeata*), found in the lower intertidal zone under rocks in tide pools. The brittle star snares food with its long arms and brings the food to its mouth in the "disc" at the center of its body. The large, yellowish northern basket star, (*Gorgonocephalus arcticus*) has five sturdy arms that divide into two branches near the center of the star, then divide again five or more times. At night, the basket star will untangle its arms to catch floating plankton in the water.

Some of the sea stars, like the smooth red cushion star (*Ceramaster granularis*), orange northern sea star (*Asterias rubens*), and the darker brown common sea star (*Asterias forbesi*), look somewhat puffier than brittle stars. The rose sea star or sun star, (*Crossaster papposus*) has a flattened body with ten or more arms covered in pinkish tufts. Sea stars move about with the help of tubular "feet" on the bottom of their appendages, and they can regenerate limbs that have broken. Sea stars use their strong limbs to pry open the shells of clams, oysters, and mussels. Sea gulls like to eat stars plucked from tidal pools.

July 3

Another Echinoderm is the sand dollar, *Echinarachnius parma*. We are most familiar with just the skeleton of the sand dollar, the white bony coin that washes up on shore. When alive, the sand dollar is covered with a velvety skin of movable spines that it uses to move around, burrow in the sand, and take food particles from the water. Break open a sand dollar skeleton and you will find five "doves of peace"—the teeth of the sand dollar.

Sand Dollar

July 4

Independence Day. Throngs of people trample along the beach in search of the perfect vantage point for fireworks, but back in the dunes are terns and plovers. The pyrotechnics begin, and birds explode from their nests, illuminated by flashes of red, white, and blue. The terns leave, their cries muffled by *booms*, *oohs*, and *aahs*; some of the birds do not come back. Piping plovers abandon the neighborhood. Eggs and chicks are exposed to the weather and vulnerable to predators. The U.S. Fish and Wildlife Service recommends that fireworks launch sites be located at least three-quarters of a mile from the nearest seabird nesting or foraging area. We share our coast and the freedom to walk its shores with other creatures; our celebrations need not come at their expense.

July 5

The sound of the sea is at once more subtle and sublime than any combusting boom or crash of manufactured starbursts. Place your ear next to the opening in a large shell and hear the roaring sound of distant surf. Sure, theories have been posed to explain the phenomenon: it is the pressure of blood rushing through your ear, echoed by the shell. It is simply air flowing through the shell, or outside noise being amplified by the size and shape of the shell. But do any of these explanations account for just how much the noise sounds like the sea? Listen—you can hear waves crashing on the beach, the high cry of a sea gull, sand grains salting into dunes, and foam dissolving as the waves recede.

July 6

Put your nose to the shell. Perhaps it smells faintly of brine, or some fragment of animal left inside to dry and rot, an odor reminiscent of mud flats and salt marshes at low tide. Marine bacteria feast on the mud and plants, breaking down organic matter into its components, particles of carbon and nutrients that then become the building blocks for new growth. As the bacteria do their thing, dimethyl sulfide gas is produced, which to us smells like salty rotting eggs, stranded seaweed, an almost empty shell.

The scent of the sea is carried on the sea breeze, which blows off the ocean toward land. On summer days, the land radiates heat more than the ocean. Warm air above the land rises, and cooler sea air rushes in to fill the void.

July 7

Salt marshes have zones based on the tides. Cordgrass (*Spartina alterniflora*) is a halophyte, a salt-loving plant that has adapted to being flooded with seawater, and grows in the lower parts of marshes that are regularly saturated by the tides. Higher marshes that are flooded infrequently are dominated by a cowlicked carpet of salt-meadow hay (*Spartina patens*). The transition zone between the two approximates the mean high-water line; the high marsh is only flooded during extreme high tides. Taller cordgrass will line the seaward edges of marshes and grow along creek banks; a shorter form of the same species grows on top of the low marsh.

Much of what we know about salt marshes in New England began with Alfred C. Redfield, who studied the marshes in Barnstable, Massachusetts, near his home on Cape Cod. Redfield was part of a scientific family: his great-grandfather was the first president of the American Association for the Advancement of Science; his grandfather was a botanist; his father, a naturalist photographer. In the spring of 1972, Alfred Redfield published a 35-page paper in the journal *Ecological Monographs* that explained how marsh development is influenced by the tides. (Redfield also discovered that the elements nitrogen, phosphorus, and carbon exist in marine life in the same proportions as in the sea: for every atom of phosphorus there are 15 atoms of nitrogen and 105 atoms of organic carbon. In their biochemistry, plants and animals mimic the ocean around them, and so Redfield said that, "Life in the sea cannot be understood without understanding the sea itself." The so-called Redfield Ratio helped oceanographers understand the marine carbon cycle, an effort that continues to this day.)

In southern Maine and along the coasts of New Hampshire and Massachusetts, extensive salt marshes occur behind barrier beaches and along the mouths of tidal rivers. Wells National Estuarine Research Reserve in Maine, Great Bay Estuary in New Hampshire, the marshes of Plum Island Sound, Massachusetts, along the Essex, Ipswich, Parker, and Rowley rivers, and the marshes on the north shore of Cape Cod are the most extensive in the Gulf of Maine. Some of these marshes are more than 5,000 years old. To the north, marshes become smaller and younger, but together the thousands of small salt marshes north of Portland make up more than half of Maine's total marsh area.

Marshes are incredibly productive environments, rivaling the richest cornfields in their production of organic matter. The organic matter and nutrients fuel a diverse food web, including the young of many commercially important fish and crustaceans.

Fiddler Crab

July 8

Animals of the intertidal zone also are adapted to the alternate wet and dry conditions created by the tide. Their internal clocks are set to the rhythm of the tide, which is the dominant physical force in their environment. For example, in the southern Gulf of Maine, fiddler crabs come out of their burrows in mud flats and creek banks at low tide to look for food. The color spots on the crab's shell contract or expand according to the sun, so that when the crab comes out of hiding he is camouflaged. The male fiddler crab has an oversized claw, which he waves in the air to attract female crabs to his burrow: *pick me! pick me!* The large claw is also used as a weapon against enemies. His name comes from the way he eats: he brings food from the ground to his mouth with his small claw, and the movement looks like he is striking a bow across a fiddle (the large claw). Three species of fiddler crabs (in the genus *Uca*) live on the east coast of North America, but they only extend as far north as Scituate, Massachusetts. Fiddler crabs release their eggs on the high tide of the full or new moon, to ensure the eggs travel to the estuary, where they will mature before returning to the marsh as juveniles on the next flood tide.

July 9

The dog days of summer have nothing to do with canine panting; they are named for Sirius, the Dog Star, which now rises with the sun. Ancient Egyptians and Romans believed that this bright star, working in concert with the sun, must be responsible for the midsummer heat. Sirius is one of the brightest stars in the sky, and is in the constellation Canis Major, one of the dogs of Orion the hunter.

July 10

By this point in the summer, spiny dogfish have completed their northern migration and have reached the western Gulf of Maine. *Squalus acanthias* is actually a small gray shark with two dorsal fins. Spiny dogfish live on both sides of the Atlantic, and are common from Nova Scotia to North Carolina. They spend the summer in the Gulf of Maine but move offshore and south for the winter. They eat whatever fish, squid, and other food is available.

Dogfish have a long, slow life cycle, with females not reproducing until they reach eight years of age. And they give birth to *live* young, an average of six pups eight to 12 inches long.

In the early twentieth century, dogfish were caught for their livers, which contain vitamin A. Synthetic vitamins were invented, and the fishery slowed. The "obnoxiously abundant" dogfish have a nasty reputation among fishermen: they crowd nets meant for more desirable fish like cod and haddock. Roving bands of hungry dogfish thrash through schools of herring and mackerel. The sharp spines on their backs make them hard to handle on the boat. But over the past twenty years, as other species have declined in numbers, a commercial fishery for dog-fish has re-emerged. While not popular eating in our area, the Brits use spiny dogfish for their fish and chips, and Germans pair beer with pickled dogfish belly—dogfish jerky.

Spiny Dogfish

July 11

"Summertime, oh, summertime, pattern of life indelible, the fade-proof lake, the woods unshatterable, the pasture with the sweetfern and the juniper forever and ever, summer without end; this was the background, and the life along the shore was the design, the cottagers with their innocent and tranquil design, their tiny docks with the flagpole and the American flag floating against the white clouds in the blue sky, the little paths over the roots of the trees leading from camp to camp and the paths to the outhouses and the can of lime for sprinkling, and at the souvenir counters at the store the miniature birch-bark canoes and the postcards that showed things looking a little better than they looked."

So wrote E. B. White in "Once More to the Lake" about his childhood summers in Belgrade, Maine. White was born in Mt. Vernon, New York, on this day in 1899. White later moved to Brooklin on the coast of Maine, where he wrote for the *New Yorker* magazine and wrote the children's classics *Charlotte's Web* and *Stuart Little*.

July 12

Writer, philosopher, and naturalist Henry David Thoreau was born on this day in 1817 in Concord, Massachusetts. A graduate of Harvard University, Thoreau was encouraged by Ralph Waldo Emerson to publish his essays and poems. He spent two years in a cabin at Walden Pond, where he went "to live deliberately, to front only the essential facts of life." Thoreau then passed on the essential facts that nature has to teach us in his many writings.

Thoreau described the ocean as savage, unfamiliar, unwearied, illimitable. Clearly he was not as at home on the beach as he was in the woods. He wrote of Cape Cod, "The sea-shore is a sort of neutral ground, a most advantageous point from which to contemplate this world. It is even a trivial place. The waves forever rolling to the land are too far-traveled and untamable to be familiar. Creeping along the endless beach amid the sun-squawl and the foam, it occurs to us that we, too, are the product of sea slime."

Today is also the birthday of the artist Andrew Wyeth, who was born in Pennsylvania but summered on the Maine coast, and whose paintings hang alongside those of his father, N. C. Wyeth, and his son, Jamie Wyeth, in the Farnsworth Art Museum in Rockland, Maine.

July 13

The salt-spray rose is blooming now, purplish-pink or white five-petaled blossoms on prickly thorn-covered stems. *Rosa rugosa* can tolerate ocean spray, and so is the rose found closest to the coast, although it is not native and has a tendency to spread aggressively in some areas. Another pink flower of the beach is the crepe-papery rose mallow (*Hibiscus moscheutos*), which grows in Massachusetts and has appeared in New Hampshire. Rose mallow can also be white with a red center.

Salt-Spray Rose

July 14

The rose-colored crust or splotch on rocks in deep tidal pools and the seafloor along rocky coasts is really a type of marine plant known as calcareous red algae or corallines. In hard-bottom areas reached by light, coralline algae are among the most abundant marine organisms. No other marine algae occupy so broad a range of habitats, from just below the tidal zone (they do not like to dry out) to depths of 700 feet, where only one-tenth of one percent of sunlight reaches these deepest of bottom-growing plants.

They grow slowly and in a variety of forms, as crusts and coatings and as unattached marls, branches, and nodules. Other algae can smother corallines, but grazing by herbivores and tumbling by waves keeps the corallines clean and healthy. Only a few animals, including chitons, limpets, and sea urchins, are able to digest the rigid, calcareous corallines. Fossil records show that coralline algae first appeared over 300 million years ago, and they have evolved to become more abundant and diverse than ever before, according to Dr. Robert Steneck of the University of Maine, who has studied the taxonomy, ecology, and evolution of coralline algae around the world.

July 15

Mountains are worn away by wind and rain, and wash into the sea. Polished by waves, the remnants of mountains are deposited at your feet. Yet the sand beneath your toes is alive. The miniature neighborhood of spaces among individual sand grains is populated by tiny creatures collectively known as "interstitial fauna": insects and tiny crustaceans, microscopic worms, and bacteria. Plowing through the sand are other animals who create their own space. Sand crabs (also called mole crabs, *Emerita talpoida*) are about an inch and a half long, sandy-colored, backward-darting crabs of the southern Gulf of Maine. They advance up the beach with the tide, and can be grasped or dug from the sand between the waves.

July 16

The more you look at a patch of sand, the more you will find. A healthy beach teems with life, strewn with algae and animals in various stages of life and death. Beneath the wrack line of stranded seaweed are sand fleas (*Platorchestia platensis*), small reddish-brown amphipod crustaceans with seven pairs of legs. Another species, *Orchestia grillus*, lives among salt-marsh grasses. Scuds are greenish amphipods that prefer tide pools and seaweed zones. These creatures and ones that are invisible to our eyes help to break down the material that gets deposited on the beach. Clearing away debris so the beach looks "clean" starves the animals who live there, and deprives us of understanding the true nature of the beach.

July 17

Take a square foot of beach home with you and make a sand candle. Place some of the damp sand in the bottom of a bucket or other container. Add a glass jar, vase, or shell—any object you want to form the mold into which the wax is poured. Fill the space around it with sand. The sand needs to be damp enough so that when you remove the object the mold holds its shape. At this point, you can press shells or other objects into the walls of the mold to leave an impression on the outside of the candle. Wrap wicking around a stick or pencil and suspend it over the mold. Carefully pour melted candle wax into the mold and let it set overnight. Remove the candle, trim the wick, and brush away any excess sand.

July 18

The July full moon is the Buck Moon, because male deer are now sprouting new antlers in anticipation of mating season, or the Thunder Moon, because summer thunderstorms start to roll across the landscape about now. As many as 2,000 thunderstorms are in progress around the world at any one moment. A thunderstorm forms when the air closest to the earth is warmer and less dense than surrounding air. The warm air rises and water vapor condenses into droplets that form clouds and rain. When the storms seem to come marching in a long, steady line, they are called squalls. Squall lines can produce hail, heavy rainfall, and weak tornadoes. Most people do not think about rain over the ocean, but all that influx of fresh water can make a difference. Hurricane Isabel dumped 400 *trillion* tons of water into the ocean before making landfall at South Carolina in 2003.

July 19

Another name for this month's moon is the Hay Moon. Marshes like those in Hampton, New Hampshire, and Ipswich, Massachusetts, were valuable sources of hay for early New England farmers, and indeed the marshes of Plum Island Sound are still harvested for salt-marsh hay, which is nutritious food for livestock. Traditionally, haying began in late summer on a low tide before the dew dried. The grass was left on the marshes to dry, and was then stacked on wooden platforms called staddles. Staddles were placed throughout the marsh and set above the tide, like haystacks on stilts. Each haystack held up to two tons of hay and stood up to 12 feet above the staddle. The hay was removed in the winter after the ground froze, and transported with horse-drawn sleds. Marsh haying has been immortalized in the paintings of Martin Johnson Heade and the poems of Nova Scotia writer John Frederic Herbin.

July 20

The sea urchin spawns during the full moons of spring and summer, shedding eggs and sperm into the water. The green sea urchin (*Strongylocentrotus droebachiensis*) is covered with short, dense spines and is full of creamy, bright yellow-orange roe in five sections. The roe is eaten as *uni* in sushi restaurants. Green sea urchins have a retractable jaw known as "Aristotle's lantern." The urchin uses five pyramid-shaped teeth inside the jaw to feed on kelp and other plants. After urchins die, their empty and spineless shells, known as tests, may be found along beaches.

Sea urchin

July 21
"I have seen horizons...."

These were the last words written by Ruth Moore, who was born on this day in 1903 on Gott's Island, two miles off the coast of Maine. She lived on the island until high school. She published fourteen novels, all of which center on life in the Maine coastal communities that she knew so well. She wrote of the tensions between locals and foreigners, between islanders and mainlanders, between working class and middle class. She has been described as a "sensitive observer" and "one of our best realists, who wrote of families whose lives depended on the sea and what it gave them." Moore had a sense of humor, which is best revealed by reading her ballads and poems with a proper Downeast accent.

July 22
A hitchhiking triggerfish was picked up at Brown's Wharf in Boothbay Harbor, Maine, on a day in July not too long ago. The triggerfish, which normally only wanders as far as Rhode Island, probably rode north on the warm currents of the Gulf Stream. If wind, temperature, and salinity conditions are right, warm, spiraling eddies may form in the Gulf Stream, carrying tropical hitchhikers to northern waters. You might find yourself swimming with a triggerfish, an iridescent butterfly fish from Caribbean reefs, or a long-nosed green garfish.

July 23

"A barnacle is nothing more than a little shrimp-like animal standing on its head in a limestone house and kicking food into its mouth." —Harvard biologist Louis Agassiz

Acorn barnacles (*Semibalanus balanoides*) are abundant in the upper intertidal zone of exposed and semiexposed rocky shores. Rockbound barnacles along the coast spend the early part of their lives as free-swimming, shrimpy individuals before they settle on rocks and pilings, shed their legs, and grow cone-shaped shells. Once committed to spending the rest of their lives glued in place, adult barnacles will call juveniles to join them, perhaps by communicating with chemical scent, or making clicking sounds. The colony grows into a rough white reef of kicking crustaceans. If the barnacles begin to outgrow the space available, they will start growing vertically on top of one another, forming rounded mounds. These barnacle hummocks are rarely found in regions of high human foot traffic because trampling easily damages them.

July 24

Like all crustaceans, a barnacle must shed its skin in order to grow. The animal sheds its thin exoskeleton and kicks it out the top hatch of the outer shell, which itself is permanent and grows with the animal. Barnacles also are preyed upon by dog whelks; the dead shells are easily broken off the rocks, and these and shed exoskeletons can wash up on shore in tinkling windrows.

The dog whelk, *Nucella lapillus,* lays its rice-shaped eggs in neat rows under rock ledges in the intertidal zone. The egg cases of another kind of whelk, the waved whelk, are called "fisherman's soap" because they produce a lathery secretion when rubbed with water. These eggs are found on the stalks of kelp.

July 25

Empty whelk shells may be inhabited by hermit crabs. Five species of hermit crabs live in the Gulf of Maine. In addition to their borrowed shells, hermit crabs may carry a fuzzy coating of "snail fur." Snail fur looks like pinkish moss or algae but is in fact a colony of animals called hydroids (*Hydractinia echinata*). Hydroids are in the same family as sea anemones, Cnidaria, a name derived from the Greek word cnidos, which means stinging nettle. Stinging nettles of the sea, cnidarians all have stinging cells on folded threadlike tentacles that they whip at zooplankton. Stunned or killed outright, the zooplankton make easy prey. Cnidarians take a variety of shapes and colors. The frilled anemone (*Metridium senile*) seems to wear a spreading crown of creamy ostrich feathers, which it directs downstream in moderate to slow currents of subtidal and low intertidal habitats. The tiny transparent white ghost anemone (*Diadumene leucolena*) lives in estuaries. The gray aggregate anemone (*Anthopleura elegantissima*) forms dense mats on seaward-facing rocks in the intertidal zone.

July 26

Hermit crabs are actually more closely related to lobsters than crabs. The American lobster (*Homarus americanus*) is found only along the eastern coast of North America from Labrador to North Carolina. At no time is the lobster more ubiquitous than in summer, when every seafood shack and restaurant flies a flag emblazoned with the red crustacean. What's not to love about the lobster? They are plentiful and profitable for fishermen, yet affordable and tasty for consumers. Lobsters make good book subjects and titles. They are a symbol of independent, self-managed fishing communities and working waterfronts, where men and women still take to the sea each morning and haul traps by hand. Young people compete for apprenticeships and spend summers as sternmen, earning cash for college. Ultimately, lobsters mean work, as the poet Leo Connellan wrote: "Lobster…my own life is in the lines hauling you in."

A lobster on your plate lived for at least six years before it was trapped, hauled on board, and sold to a dealer or lobster pound. Your lobster dinner is probably a male or an immature female, because females are now ripe with eggs and thus are left in the sea to reproduce. If a Maine lobsterman catches a "berried" female, he punches a V-shaped notch in her tail so that others will know she is a fertile female. The only times that lobstering is prohibited is at night from June through October, and on Sundays during the summer tourist season.

July 27

Three thousand years ago, ancestors of the Passamaquoddy Tribe of Native Americans etched images of animals, people, and shaman figures into the shale ledges of Maine's Machias Bay. The Picture Rock site is the largest concentration of petroglyphs on the East Coast, and is now preserved by the Passamaquoddy Tribe with the assistance of Maine Coast Heritage Trust.

July 28

The Delta Aquarid meteor shower falls around this time, radiating from Delta Aquarii, one of the brightest stars in the constellation Aquarius. Unlike most meteor showers, the source of these shooting stars is unknown.

July 29

Now that trumpet flower and foxglove blooms tumble like stars from Aquarius' urns, ruby-throated hummingbirds are seen more often. At three and a half inches long and weighing a tenth of an ounce (less than a penny), *Archilochus colubris* are the smallest birds in northeastern North America and the only birds that can fly backward. Their wings are capable of beating seventy times per second (and their hearts ten), sending a vibrating buzz through your soul, demanding attention as they dart and hover in pursuit of nectar. They are miniature humming chandeliers, with feathers of crystals that refract sunlight into red and green jewel tones.

July 30

The sea has its own sources of gemlike hues, yielding their essence only reluctantly. Take, for example, the pearly substance that lends glittery sheen to cosmetics, paint, and jewelry: it comes from the scales of herring. A byproduct of the herring fishery and once a major industry in some places like Eastport, Maine, pearl essence is made by putting scales through a chemical process that uses solvents to wash out the "pearl"—really a substance called guanin. Synthetic substitutes are now favored over natural pearl essence, which is no longer produced in the U.S.

July 31

Oysters, clams, and mussels can form pearls when the inside of their shells becomes irritated, as by a grain of sand. The mollusk secretes nacre, a mineral compound that in some species takes on a pearly luster. The nacre is released in a series of layers, and the chemistry of the surrounding water can influence the developing pearl's color. Historically, most gem pearls came from oysters in the Persian Gulf. Nacre is also the substance that coats the inner surface of shells (mother-of-pearl), and we do still take things from the sea solely for this beautiful material. In the U.S., oyster-shell products and mussel-shell buttons are part of a $60 billion ocean products industry.

BEACH WALK SOUVENIR

Never as bright the stones
      we find, the stones we stoop
            to gather, all slick with the sea

and its tossing glimmer—
      no matter how we turn
            to burnish them again in our palms

or pocket them
      (even in our mouths)
            something in their gleam is gone

or left with whatever's flashing
      back in the sand: centuries
            of salt tumbling stones out of time

and licking every trick made
      of light, leaving us to question
            what entices us, what lasts.

Candice Stover
Mount Desert, Maine

August

August 1

"It had been a perfect August day on the coast of Maine, one of those few late summer days with no fog or even any haze. The waters of Frenchman Bay sparkled brilliantly in the sunlight, the leaves of the deciduous trees stirred ever so sensuously in the slight warm breeze. Many summer folk had gone a-sailing. A few crossbills had been spotted on the West Side of Taunton Point; and the annual tennis tournament was in full swing."

Maine writer Sanford Phippen's nostalgic if somewhat tongue-in-cheek description of a perfect midsummer day on the coast captures the quintessential August: the frenetic pace of early summer is a distant memory, the leaves are a full if duller green, the grasses are going to seed, and the Gulf of Maine is finally warm enough for swimming (maybe). You will know high summer has arrived when the cicadas and crickets begin to sing and tourists have settled in as if they own the place. In his short stories and novels, Phippen confronts the friction between his native Downeast and visitors and newcomers, reminding us that "Maine is not all gracious summer cottages with noble lobstermen on every pier. There's a dark side that either gets glossed over or totally left out or over-romanticized." It is easy in these perfect summer days to romanticize coastal living, but it is worth remembering the hard work that makes enjoying this time possible, wherever you spend your seasons.

August 2

Taking time to reflect allows the August panic to settle in: thoughts of all the summer activities that remain undone, the ones that will never be attempted. Give up on all your big plans and watch the season pass, accept the summer for what it has become. Rain brings the smell of ripe fruit rotting, flowers fading. The marshes begin to pale, the sea continues to warm. Here and there a leaf may turn yellow, a seedpod may pop. The days are noticeably shorter. Time never moves as fast, is felt as fast, as in August.

August 3

Spiders and caterpillars seem to multiply; on Warren Island in Penobscot Bay is a red-spotted, white-tufted, black caterpillar, the larva of the whitemarked tussock moth, one of the nine or so species of stinging caterpillars in the Northeast. A stinging caterpillar? Strange but true. All stinging caterpillars have hairs that can irritate the skin. They leave an itchy sting, like fine cactus spines or nettles, and a rash may develop. They are colorful beasts with strange appendages, some with luxurious coats of tan fur (like the unattractively named "puss caterpillar"), others with tufts of stinging hairs that they shoot at unsuspecting victims. The key is to avoid touching any unfamiliar caterpillar that has hairs or spines.

August 4

One caterpillar you *can* pick up (gently) is the luna moth caterpillar, a big, fat, green caterpillar with a light brown head and moving mouth parts. You can watch him munch on birch leaves. Soon, he will wrap himself up in a leaf cocoon. If it is late, he may wait until next spring to experience metamorphosis, and emerge as a large, pale-green luna moth. Adult luna moths (*Actias luna*) live for only one week, making observations of these ephemeral winged creatures special and rare. Look for them at night clinging to window screens illuminated by lights or a full moon.

August 5

Beachcombing is the word we use for walking along the beach, eyes downward, scanning the tide line for prized shells, sea glass, stones, messages in bottles, anything that catches the eye. There is no limit to what could wash up on the beach. The best time to beachcomb is after a big storm, when wind and strong waves have cast deep-hidden items upon the shore. After a spring or monthly high tide is good, too, and remember to go early in the morning, for large or highly valued items are picked up by the first person who happens to come along. Beachcombing offers meditation because you are so focused on the narrow strip of sand in front of you and your peripheral vision is filled with sun reflecting off waves and sand. It is a relaxing exercise but one that requires concentration. Perhaps you are searching for your past, a clue to your ancestry, some familiar fragment that has meaning only you understand. Or maybe you seek the aboriginal space described by John Burroughs, of being on the edge, at the mercy of an ocean larger and older than you, an ocean that takes what we throw away and throws it back at our feet, polished and worn, an ocean from which you, like all of us, were born.

August 6

While beachcombing you may come across a piece of wood that is filled with holes, the telltale signs of shipworms (*Teredo navalis*). Shipworms are actually a type of mollusk that first bores into wood as larvae, and then grows up to two feet long. Adult shipworms have a small shell on their head which they use to burrow through wood, forming a maze of round tunnels. The shipworm then eats the wood it has cut away. Multiple shipworms in one piece of wood will avoid each other, twisting and turning their tunnels, eventually weakening whatever wooden structure they have invaded to the point of collapse.

Every year, shipworms cause an estimated $1 billion in damage to wooden boats, shipwrecks, and marine structures like docks and pilings. Over the years, humans found ways to fight back against the boring shipworms, but many of these methods involved toxic substances like creosote and copper arsenate. New techniques and materials such as fiber-reinforced composites are proving effective against the borers. At the same time, however, cleaner, warmer waters are allowing *Teredo navalis* to spread north more rapidly.

August 7

Jellyfish are sometimes stranded on the beach. The most commonly seen jelly of late summer is the moon jelly (*Aurelia aurita*), a milky white jellyfish with a cloverleaf design on its top. The moon jelly does not sting and swims near the surface in coastal waters.

The lion's mane jelly (*Cyanea capillata*) can grow up to six feet long. Beneath its brownish bell or "mane" dangle eight clusters, each with 150 stinging tentacles.

Jellyfish compensate for being mostly water with their tentacles, which are covered with stinging cells that they shoot like harpoons whenever they brush up against something. Jellyfish are Cnidarians, related to anemones and hydroids, and most fall into the class Scyphozoa, of which there are at least 16 species documented for the Gulf of Maine. Many are deep-water jellyfish that are unlikely to be seen on the beach. These include the egg-yolk jelly (*Phacellophora camtschatica*), a large jelly that looks like an egg cracked into boiling water; the helmet jelly (*Periphylla periphylla*); and *Atolla wyvillei*, a reddish, crown-shaped jelly.

Nanomia cara are similar to jellyfish but are in a different class and are related to the Portuguese man-of-war. They form string-like colonies and swim in deeper water. In past years, the organism has occurred in sufficient abundance within the Gulf of Maine to foul the nets of commercial fishermen.

August 8

Young butterfish like to swim among the tentacles of the lion's mane jellyfish. The butterfish (*Peprilus triacanthus*) is a small, flat fish with pointed fins and a forked tail. The belly is silvery, the sides pale, and the back a bluish gray. They prefer sandy bottom areas but stay near the surface in estuaries and bays, traveling in small bands or schools. Butterfish are regular summer visitors to the Gulf, especially off the Massachusetts coast. Butterfish are reportedly good eating, and sound like it, but really their name comes from the slippery mucus that coats their scales. This mucus protects juvenile butterfish from jellyfish stings, a welcome defense for a young fish who likes to take cover underneath floating jellies.

August 9

In recent years, some parts of the world's ocean have experienced increased numbers of jellyfish. Many scientists believe this is a result of human influence on the ocean that is disrupting the balance of the marine food web and creating ideal conditions for jellyfish to thrive: few predators (not as many big fish and sea turtles) and plenty of food (algae, fueled by nutrients running off the land). While this is a somewhat simplified explanation for observed "blooms" of jellyfish, here in the Gulf of Maine we have what some believe to be our own example of marine disruption.

In the past twenty years, a green seaweed has appeared in the waters and on the beaches of Cobscook Bay near Eastport, Maine. The green slime is an alga called *Enteromorpha intestinalis*. In some parts of Cobscook Bay, the alga forms a solid mat that stretches out into the distance. Sometimes it forms long, twisted ropes. Several people have said it looks like a golf course, but up close, at the water's edge or in a tide pool, *Enteromorpha* looks and feels like hollow strands of slippery green tissue. The cause of these *Enteromorpha* blooms is not known.

August 10

Another green, tissue-thin macroalga is sea lettuce (*Ulva lactuca*). Pieces of sea lettuce float in tide pools and at the water's edge, although it can also attach to rocks. This bright-green alga is only two cells thick and is easily torn and difficult to press; it readily disintegrates when dry. Sea lettuce grows fast, and like *Enteromorpha* it is sometimes considered to be an indicator of high nutrient levels. Sea lettuce is edible.

August 11

Louise Bogan was born on August 11, 1897, in Livermore Falls, Maine. Her father was a millworker and she spent a turbulent childhood among the Irish communities of working-class New England. She lived many places as an adult and eventually stayed in New York City, but, as with many poets, the coast continued to creep into her work. Here, an excerpt from one of her later poems, "Night":

The cold remote islands
    And the blue estuaries
        Where what breathes, breathes
The restless wind of the inlets,
    And what drinks, drinks
        The incoming tide....

August 12

Fire in the sky: mid-August brings the Perseid meteor shower. At its peak, as many as one or two balls of fire may streak through the sky each minute. Perseids are space-rock fragments of the Swift-Tuttle comet, and each year about this time the earth crosses the path of the comet's tail. The Perseids seem to originate from the constellation Perseus, which is below Cassiopeia and the Big Dipper, now high in the northern sky. In Greek mythology, Perseus was the son of Zeus and the hero who killed the snake-haired Medusa.

The Perseid is one of the best meteor showers to watch, since the night is warm enough to lie on a dark beach far from the glare of city lights, at the edge of a midnight sea, with all the universe before your eyes.

August 13

Fire at sea: Saint Elmo's fire is a bluish-white glow that appears in the wake of thunderstorms. Ship masts may appear to be on fire, burning like candles. Saint Elmo's fire has been described by Columbus, Magellan, Shakespeare, Melville, and Charles Darwin. During a thunderstorm, the air tenses with electric energy a thousand times stronger than during fair weather. Electrons from the charged air collide with pointed objects like masts and church steeples, and the released light energy concentrates around the point and glows with a heatless flame that is sometimes accompanied by a hissing or sizzling sound. This is a technical if sketchy description. In reality, the sight of Saint Elmo's fire has inspired tales of spiritual intervention and magic. Mariners have traditionally interpreted Saint Elmo's fire as a good omen, because it usually means that a storm is nearly over. The name of Saint Elmo is attributed to an Italian derivation of Sant 'Ermo or St. Erasmus, and St. Elmo is the patron saint of sailors.

August 14

Fire on the horizon: the green flash. Another natural phenomenon involving light, the green flash occurs when the sun slips below the horizon. Refraction increases at shorter wavelengths. The sun sets, taking with it the longer red and orange light. Shorter wavelengths of light then bend around the horizon and linger for a few seconds, appearing to our eyes as a flash of green.

August 15

Fire on the ground: if the summer has been dry, the danger of
wildfires may be heightened. In the Gulf of Maine, some landscapes are more vulnerable to fire than others, in part because
they have adapted to periodic burning. Chief among these are
the pitch pine–oak barrens of Cape Cod and Plymouth County,
Massachusetts, and southern Maine.

Pine barrens occur on acidic, well-drained sandy soils
of the coastal plain in southern New England, Long Island, and
New Jersey, as well as in more limited inland areas on glacial
sand plains and shallow mountain soils on ridgetops. The pines
and oaks and heathlike shrubs evolved to grow in low-nutrient
conditions, although "barren" is not the right word for these
forests, as they provide habitat for a number of rare plants and
animals. For example, 30 percent of the butterflies and moths
of conservation concern in New England and New York require
scrub oak to host their larvae.

Pitch pine bark is thick and flaky, with lots of air spaces,
and the trees can survive being consumed by flames, which used
to occur naturally about every twenty-five years. The oils and
waxes in the leaves of pitch pine, scrub oak, and shrubs like
huckleberry and blueberry help to sustain fires, so that they
burn even when plants are green. Fire suppression has actually
increased the risk of damaging wildfire in areas of pine-oak
forest, because without periodic burning, fuels build up to
dangerous levels that can be difficult to control. Fires eliminate
flame-intolerant trees and plants, maintaining the pine–oak
ecosystem and the disturbed habitat needed by certain species,
including the flower northern blazing star, birds such as night-
jars and whippoorwills, and black racer snakes.

August 16

The August full moon is called the Green Corn Moon, Grain Moon, or Sturgeon Moon. Two species of sturgeon live in the Gulf of Maine, the Atlantic sturgeon (*Acipenser oxyrinchus oxyrinchus*) and the shortnose sturgeon (*Acipenser brevirostrum*). Sturgeon are prehistoric creatures, having been around for 100 million years, since the era of the dinosaurs. Both species historically ranged along the East Coast between Canada and the St. Johns River in Florida, but many populations have disappeared due to pollution and overfishing. Sturgeon were harvested for food and for caviar in the twentieth century. Shortnose sturgeon were listed as endangered in 1967 (before the Endangered Species Act), and the status of Atlantic sturgeon is under review. Atlantic sturgeon are a late-maturing species that can grow up to 14 feet long; they move out to sea for several years before returning to fresh water to spawn in the spring. Shortnose sturgeon remain in estuaries as adults, dwelling on the bottom and eating small crustaceans and fish from the mud flats. Shortnose sturgeon spend the winter huddled together in deep pools.

August 17

At some point in summer we come across a newspaper headline like BEACHES REOPEN AFTER SHARK SIGHTINGS. One August, officials in Wells, Maine, closed the town's beaches after sharks were spotted offshore and a dead mako shark washed up at the Wells Beach jetty. Shark sightings are rare in Maine, as the fish usually stay far out at sea, but they may follow smaller fish toward shore if the water is warm.

One of the shark sightings in Wells was of a basking shark, which is a filter feeder. Its scientific name, *Cetorhinus maximus*, means "ocean monster with a big nose" in Greek. The common name comes from their habit of sunning themselves at the surface, with first dorsal fin fully exposed. Docile and completely uninterested in humans, basking sharks are typically seen swimming slowly at the surface, mouth agape in open water near shore. Hundreds of tiny, backward-curving teeth line the bulky head, poised to strain tiny zooplankton from the ocean. Up to 2,000 tons of water may pass through the basking shark's mouth *each hour*. Our second largest shark after the whale shark, the basking shark can grow up to 35 feet long. The largest specimen, 40 feet long and weighing 16 tons, was trapped in a herring net in the Bay of Fundy in 1851. The basking shark is found around the world; it is considered endangered in the North Atlantic.

Other shark species that frequent the Gulf of Maine include mako, porbeagle, blue, thresher, spiny dogfish, and the (rare) great white shark. Porbeagles and blue sharks are smaller but move inshore in August to feed on stripers and bluefish. In a warm year, higher water temperatures will stimulate blooms of algae that attract smaller fish like mackerel, which in turn attract sharks, which in turn scare the heck out of vacationing beachgoers. There has never been a confirmed shark attack anywhere in Maine or New Hampshire, and there have been only four confirmed attacks in Massachusetts, according to the University of Florida's International Shark Attack File. Despite newspaper headlines, a visitor to a U.S. beach is more likely to perish in a collapsing sand hole than be killed by a shark.

August 18

Presumed shark sightings might actually be observations of other finned creatures such as dolphins and porpoises, or the wobbling fin of an ocean sunfish. *Mola mola* looks like a head with fins; she moves by wiggling her top and bottom fins, using her blunt, folded tail as a rudder. She rolls about near the surface, perhaps on her side, eating jellyfish and other drifting flotsam. A bit of a klutz and kind of awkward, the sunfish is a gentle giant. The ocean sunfish is the heaviest bony fish in the world (they can weight up to 5,000 pounds!). She carries hundreds of millions of eggs, which hatch into tiny, spike-covered puffed fish that quickly grow and flatten into the thick, rounded slab of an adult Mola.

August 19

Like beachcombing, tide-pooling is an activity in which we go down to the water's edge to see what we can see. The great thing about both is that the experience is never the same twice. Each pool is different, and contains its own assemblage of organisms. By what chance does one pool fill with inflated green algae and the other with clumps of brown moss animals? In this one, a sea star. A few feet away, a colony of snails. The longer you look, the more you see. Suddenly, the tide pool becomes an entire ocean, an ecosystem unto itself, until a sea gull's cry interrupts your trance and you look up, the moment erased by the brilliant sun glaring off the rocks.

Tide Pool

A few hundred feet down the beach, a gaggle of children is crawling over the rocks. They seem to toddle, but they are sure-footed, venturing all the way to the edge, to where the rocks are slippery with seaweed and black cyanobacteria, where the ocean splashes on their brightly colored clothing. The little people are in constant motion, their adult chaperones casually behind them. They hop and waver, one catches her own fall with her hands, another pauses to catch his balance. Back and forth over the rocks, like a tottering rainbow of marbles rolling to a stop. They, too, are tide-pooling, for children more so than adults seem to appreciate the microcosm of a tide pool.

August 20

One thing to keep in mind about tide pools is that they are not touch tanks in place for your sole entertainment. Do not remove organisms from the tide pool and take them home—they will die in that bucket. Transferring organisms from one pool to another disrupts the harmony of both pools. If you turn over a rock or shell to see what is underneath, put it back the way you found it. If an animal does not want to budge, don't yank on it. Sea star arms will not grow back before your eyes so do not break them off. The best approach is to crouch on the rim of the pool and just watch for a while. Dip your hand in the water slowly, and be nice. (Good advice for lots of situations....)

August 21

If you stare into a tide pool long enough you may see a tiny, fringed, wormlike animal swimming or crawling around. This is a Nudibranch, a shell-less snail also known as a sea slug. There are over forty species of these strange, beautiful creatures in the Gulf of Maine, with exotic names like shag-rug aeolis, white Atlantic cadlina, and crown doto. They are exotically colored in order to warn predators that they may sting or secrete sulfuric acid.

August 22

We comb the beach and gaze into tide pools in search of wonder and beauty. Yet heed the lowly sea cucumber, ugly cousin of urchins and starfish, and the frequent brunt of Dave Barry jokes. But *Cucumaria frondosa* has hidden talents: he can squeeze through tiny spaces, and he can temporarily expel his innards if stressed or disturbed. He has no known predators, and he and his brothers and sisters take up a lot of space on the seafloor. He also is sought after by an increasing number of fishermen, and, if caught, he may be sold to a processor and shipped to Asia, where he is valued as food and an aphrodisiac. Go ahead and gently prod him—see what he does.

August 23

After a storm, broken pieces of finger sponges or bread crumb sponges may litter the beach. Sponges are colonial animals in the phylum Porifera. Instead of organs they have specialized cells that draw in water and food and expel wastes. Forty-two species of marine sponges have been documented from the Gulf of Maine. They range in color from white to green to yellow to orange to red.

August 24

If all this talk of cucumbers and bread crumbs makes you hungry, go find out if blueberries can still be picked in woods and fields. Lowbush blueberry (*Vaccinium angustifolium*) grows across the sandy barrens and sunny hilltops of southern and eastern Maine, and in the woods of New Hampshire and Massachusetts. Wild blueberries are harvested from over 60,000 acres in Maine, with an annual value of about $75 million. They are indeed wild; blueberry fields are maintained only by burning. These are not the fat, watery cultivated blueberries of more southerly states, but the tiny, dark fruit of woodland paths and rocky fields.

August 25

While it doesn't have any scent, sea lavender more than makes up for it with its profusion of tiny purple flowers that create a haze above salt marshes. The flowers emerge on the tips of the branched stem, which is surrounded by a rosette of thick leaves that remain flat against the marsh surface. Sea lavender (*Limonium nashii*) is used in floral arrangements, but it is not so common and can become locally scarce of too many plants are picked.

Sea Lavender

August 26

Another flower of late summer is the goldenrod. There are many species of goldenrod and they can hybridize with each other, making identification difficult. But there is no mistaking seaside goldenrod. *Solidago sempervirens* can tolerate salt spray and tidal flooding; a pioneering species, it readily grows in salt marshes and dunes. It has succulent leaves, because internal salt accumulation forces water to enter the leaf via osmosis. Yellow flowers are borne in a dense, large spray. The flowers will fade in a month or so, but the leaves will stay green through the winter, hence the *sempervirens* part of its name, which means "always green."

August 27

The crickets and cicadas that began singing at the end of July are now reaching a crescendo. Cicadas are flying, tree-sucking insects related to leafhoppers. They are big bugs with wide-set eyes and clear wings; they do not sting or bite but their buzzing action can be scary when held in the hand. Their humming is produced by the males, who vibrate special structures called tymbals on the sides of their belly. Every species of cicada has a unique call. The frequency and tone of their sound is related to the temperature and the time of day.

Annual or "dog day" cicadas (*Tibicen* species) appear every year, but periodical cicadas emerge only every thirteen or seventeen years. While these cyclic cicadas are uncommon in New England, rumor is that a brood of seventeen-year cicadas is due to arrive here soon.

August 28

The first blush on north-facing leaves is a reminder that the great shorebird migration is about to begin. Thousands of migratory shorebirds will pause on mud flats and beaches of the Gulf of Maine on their way south for the winter. One bird who passes through on his way to South America, possibly stopping to pluck tasty fiddler crabs from the marshes, is the whimbrel (*Numenius phaeopus*). The whimbrel is a large but short-legged shorebird with a long downward-curved bill, striped head, and brown-speckled body. The whimbrel is related to the Eskimo curlew (*Numenius borealis*). The Eskimo curlew was believed to be extinct, but a few unconfirmed sightings suggest otherwise. Historic flocks in the thousands were greatly reduced by hunting. Eskimo curlews were called "dough birds" because they were rich with fat when they arrived in New England. A hunter could kill dozens with a single shot, and the dispersed flock would return to the same spot to be fired upon again.

August 29

Late summer blooms of phytoplankton and zooplankton will attract many animals to feed and fatten before the winter. Blooms of red feed, the copepod *Calanus finmarchius*, are the favorite food of red-necked phalaropes. The red-necked phalarope (*Phalaropus lobatus*) is one of only three species of phalaropes worldwide, and they are the only shorebirds that would rather swim than wade and the only ones that spend the winter at sea instead of in Central or South America.

Some two million red-necked phalaropes once stopped over in the Bay of Fundy region between Maine and Canada, but their numbers have declined for unknown reasons. Phalaropes have been called "gale birds" by sailors, who expected a strong blow when phalaropes were seen congregating in the water.

Sandpiper

August 30

The sanderling (*Calidris alba*) is one of the most widespread shorebirds, found on nearly all sandy beaches throughout the world. Sanderlings fly to the Arctic to breed, but those who for whatever reason do not breed remain in South America. (Why make that long trip if you're not going to breed anyway?) A few will begin their migration but decide to stay along our coast instead. Even more will pass through again, now on their way back south. Sanderlings are similar to other small sandpipers, but they are paler with a white face, black bill and legs and a bold white wing bar that is visible when the bird is flying. They run along the tide line, pecking in the sand for food, darting in and out with the waves.

August 31

And so comes to a close August, "a month when nothing succeeds like excess," wrote John Hay, poet, naturalist, and award-winning author of many, many books of literary nonfiction about the natural world of Cape Cod and beyond, who was born on this day in 1915 in Ipswich, Massachusetts. Hay's writing urges us to watch, and listen, to participate in the great democracy of nature into which we were born. Sometimes perspective of the mind is best gained through perspective of the eye—head for somewhere high along the coast where you will be able to look out at the horizon and down upon the surf. Good vantage points are everywhere along this coast: the bold cliffs of Cutler, Maine, and the even higher cliffs of Monhegan, or the tall dunes on the great beach of Cape Cod. Perhaps, like Hay, you will surpass the boundaries that confine you, and it will begin to be an open world again. What will you take with you from this season to the next?

SEPTEMBER

And now the slow slide into autumn:
the thinning crickets, the monarchs
moving weightless among us like orange
angels, the tight-lipped rose hips;
the brown curl of aspen leaf, the bikes
tossed willy-nilly on the schoolhouse
lawn. Even the shadows slide, like blue
cloaks about the apple trees. Now
the mornings deepen; the meadow glints
of scraggle weed and thorn and a
russet splatter of barberry sweeps in
among the spruce. September, like
the hem of a dress moving easy
through the grass, and we running
alongside, tune our engines, whip-
whine our saws, rattle the storm
windows from the cellar, backhoe
our wells, wrap our buoys in their
day-glow dresses. We, running
alongside, bent on keeping pace,
our eyes focused on the road ahead,
our ears thrumming.

Jan Bailey
Monhegan, Maine

September

September 1

September arrives under the cover of lengthening night. A slight chill creeps into the morning, but by midday the sun rises high above marshes still awash in sea lavender and goldenrod. The sun is setting noticeably earlier, and evenings return to that golden hue of memory, orange streaks across the sky and sea. The Big Dipper sinks lower in the sky, now upright and capable of holding a cupful of the black night. In the water and on the shores below the stars, a myriad of changes are taking place as summer fades to autumn.

September 2

The ancient Greek philosopher Heraclitus said "nothing endures but change." The enduring change around us is what makes it possible for our world to stay the same: were it not for the changing tides, the beaches and marshes would not survive. Maine scientist and fisherman Ted Ames wrote in 1996, "Change is the most obvious constant in the sea. Its inhabitants are attuned to its timeless rhythm, and have orchestrated their life cycles to coincide with it." At no time is change more noticeable than during fall. And so September begins the drama that is autumn in the Gulf of Maine.

Goldenrod and Asters

September 3

The writer Sarah Orne Jewett was born on this day in 1849 in South Berwick, Maine, where she spent much of her life when she wasn't traveling. Jewett captured this bittersweet time of year in the final chapter of *The Country of the Pointed Firs*: "At last it was the time of late summer, when the house was cool and damp in the morning, and all the light seemed to come through green leaves; but at the first step out of doors the sunshine always laid a warm hand on my shoulder, and the clear, high sky seemed to lift quickly as I looked at it. There was no autumnal mist on the coast, nor any August fog; instead of these, the sea, the sky, all the long shore line and the inland hills, with every bush of bay and every fir-top, gained a deeper color and a sharper clearness. There was something shining in the air, and a kind of luster on the water and the pasture grass —a northern look that, except at this moment of the year, one must go far to seek. The sunshine of a northern summer was coming to its lovely end."

September 4

Now is the time to pay attention, as so much that is here will soon leave, including many of our coastal birds, who are preparing for long migrations to Central and South America. On a single night, thousands of birds may be in flight overhead as they journey south. Robert Peter Tristram Coffin, a writer from Harpswell, Maine, saw the sandpeeps and plovers as silver strung across the sky, shedding bright beads of music "so bright it is sad." You, too, can see this show, if you find a rock to sit on at the edge of a marsh or mud flat in early morning and wait for a note, a flash, of silver.

September 5

Prompted by hormones, our migratory birds are beginning to feast as the days become shorter and their appetites increase. Some birds take advantage of abundant, carbohydrate-rich bearberries, crowberries, bunchberries, cranberries; other birds like osprey and eagles seek out fish that are migrating down rivers to the sea. Energy is stored, the birds get fat, all the time waiting for just the right breeze to carry them away. The tip of a wing, and suddenly the sky is filled with the drumbeat rush of feather, wind, and time.

September 6

While you are sleeping, a river of birds is flowing in the sky above. Because they spend the daylight hours eating, many birds migrate at night, when cooler, denser air keeps them aloft with fewer flaps of wing. Birds also tend to migrate after fall rainstorms, when both clearing weather and tailwinds are favorable, allowing them to save energy on their epic journeys. However they get there—genetically encoded instructions, sunlight, starlight, or the earth's magnetic field—migrating birds find their way to wintering areas beyond the Gulf of Maine. Scientists are still researching these eternal questions of navigation, though perhaps when it comes to animals in flight, some of us prefer mystery over fact, wonderment to explanation.

September 7

Insects migrate in fall, too. When the sun drops to about 57 degrees above the southern horizon, local monarch butterflies (*Danaus plexippus*) take flight, joining a migration of millions. Monarchs from northeastern North America journey 2,500 miles to their wintering grounds in the mountain forests of central Mexico. Yet not a single one of the monarchs that are leaving now has made this journey before: they are the children and grandchildren and great-grandchildren of the butterflies

Monarch Butterflies

that flew north last spring. Somehow, they find their way southwest along the path of their ancestors, converging over Texas with other monarchs from across the eastern half of the continent. Butterflies do not fly in the rain, so look for them on sunny days near roadsides, fields, marshes, and meadows—wherever the milkweed plant grows.

September 8
During this month of movement and transition, it seems we need to be reminded that it is still summer. Even the plant world is getting ready for the cold. As the nights get longer and cooler, chemical changes within plants create the visual changes we associate with fall. But early September is only the beginning—a yellow leaf here, a brown fern there, beach grass turned to straw—signs of the changes yet to come.

September 9
Salt marshes have their own transitions. Fiddler crabs venture deeper below the marsh, and the saltwater minnows called mummichogs bury themselves in the mud at the bottom of pools and tidal creeks. The outer leaves of *Spartina* grasses, black rush, and sedges die back, even as goldenrod and asters remain in bloom. Blades of salt-meadow hay dry in stiff cowlicks across the upper marsh. As the grasses die, their old roots (actually tuber-like rhizomes) become part of the marsh peat, adding a new layer to be filled in with sediments by the tide and become the ground beneath next summer's roots.

September 10
The dying plants are contributing to a cycle that will eventually bring new life to the marsh come spring. At first, the marsh grasses like *Spartina alterniflora* remain attached to their below-ground rhizomes. But winter will break the stems, which

will become either food for a wide range of critters, or else will collect into mat-like rafts of wrack. Spring's high tides will push the rafts over and across the marsh, and some mats will be stranded as the tide leaves. The mats will decay in the hot sunlight of summer, and new grass will grow through old stems. By the end of summer only a few of the larger mats will remain on the marsh, and the now-dying grasses of autumn will supply the materials for the next spring's wrack.

September 11

As plants mature, they send forth seeds to carry on their line-age. Every species has evolved its own strategy for reproduction, some of which become apparent in late summer and early fall. In the forests, clusters of new cones have sprouted from the tops of spruces. Maples and ashes drop battalions of winged samaras. In the marshes, cattail heads turn light brown and fluffy as the seeds begin to disperse and are carried by the wind. Plantains and black rush have but empty capsules where seeds have already fallen out. Still other plants rely on animals to carry their seeds across great distances. No two reproductive structures are alike; in fact, in many plants the seed is the only way to identify the species.

cattails

September 12

Disintegrating heads of cattails (*Typha angustifolia*) can be seen in tidal marshes and along rivers, where stands of this plant mark the boundary between salt water and fresh water. Cattails can withstand the water level fluctuations created by the tides, but they will not tolerate regular saturation by marine-strength waters. They grow on the upper (inland) edges of marshes, or in a band between mud flat and riverbank. Marshes form behind barrier beaches or in protected rivers and coves where a good supply of sediment allows their development.

September 13

Less protected sections of the coast have a more abrupt boundary between land and sea. On the bluffs of downeast Maine and Boston Harbor islands, the terrestrial land cover grows right to the edge, seeming to almost spill into the sea. Spruce and cedar cling to granite ledges with stubborn roots, and a fringe of overhanging mosses softens the transition from earth to water. And so it is possible to hike in the forest and climb mountains, all the while glimpsing turquoise seas and hearing cries of gulls. Senses can be overwhelmed in such settings; being on the edge requires that you be open to the surprises that are inspired when landscapes overlap.

September 14

Trees and shrubs that grow near the ocean—on cliffs in the north and sand dunes in the south—must tolerate harsh conditions of wind and sea spray. Incessant winds prune trees into angular shapes. Bushes at the very edge get the full brunt of the wind, which stunts their growth. Shrubs and trees just beyond can grow a little taller. The side exposed to the wind dies and the sheltered side continues to grow. This pattern can be seen in the growth rings of woody dune plants, where the sheltered side of the rings is wider than the windward side. Spray-tolerant shrubs and trees have thick, waxy leaves or needles and tough bark.

September 15

The middle of September usually marks International Coastal Cleanup Day, when scores of volunteers around the world will join the Ocean Conservancy in removing trash and other debris from beaches. Marine debris is a collective term for stuff in the ocean that does not belong there, including glass, metal, wood, and plastic. Plastic bags and balloons are eaten by sea turtles and ocean sunfish, who mistake them for jellyfish. Seabirds and whales get tangled up in lost and discarded fishing gear. Plastic breaks down into microscopic spheres that are ingested by all kinds of organisms. The variety of marine debris and the ways that it can harm marine life has no end. Surveying the beach to remove debris before it washes back out to sea is a small but not insignificant way to help.

September 16

The full moon closest to the autumnal equinox is the Harvest Moon, perhaps the most stunning of all full moons when it rises at sunset, lingering huge and golden over the horizon. The Harvest Moon is so named because northern farmers who were working long days to harvest their crops before winter would continue to work in the fields by the light of the full moon. The next full moon will be the Hunter's Moon.

September 17

Some animals change their appearance as autumn nears. The black guillemot (*Cepphus grylle*) is a common, pigeon-sized seabird that nests in burrows among the rocks of Maine coastal islands such as Great Duck, Eastern Egg Rock, and Stratton. Around this time of year, guillemots lose their summer breeding plumage (black with white wing patches) and change to a mottled gray-and-brown. Found from the Arctic Circle as far south as Maine, the guillemot is our most near-shore member of the Auk family, which also includes puffins and murres. These birds fly underwater for long distances, and serve the same ecological niche as penguins in the Southern Hemisphere.

Black Guillemots

September 18

Speaking of flying underwater, three species of marine turtles inhabit the Gulf of Maine. The leatherback (*Dermochelys coriacea*) is the world's largest turtle, growing up to eight feet long and 1,500 pounds. After breeding on southern beaches, leatherbacks follow the migration of arctic jellyfish, their favorite food, to the Gulf of Maine in summer. In autumn they move back south through bays and sounds of New England.

The leatherback is federally listed as an endangered species. Both the threatened loggerhead turtle (*Caretta caretta*) and the smaller endangered Atlantic or Kemp's Ridley turtle (*Lepidochelys kempii*) wander throughout the Atlantic Ocean. These sea turtles visit the Gulf of Maine when water temperatures remain above 68°F (20°C). Ridleys use shallower water than loggerheads, hunting crabs in sea grass beds.

Loggerhead Turtle

September 19

Inland, baby snapping turtles are emerging from their buried nests in sandy roadsides, sawdust piles, and riverbanks. They now must evade hungry skunks, foxes, raccoons, and coyotes and find their way to the closest water. Snapping turtles (*Chelydra serpentina*) will take up residence in any marsh, stream, lake, or estuary. They prefer a soft, muddy bottom, slow-moving water, and marshy backwaters. While snapping turtles are placid when in water, even the little ones will get testy when on dry land. They do not care if you are simply trying to help them cross the road; if they are out of water they will snap and hiss and give you the evil eye. Help them anyway (staying well beyond the reach of their long neck and snapping jaw!).

September 20

Like snapping turtles, crows get a bad rap. It can be hard to love crows when their early morning cacophony takes place outside the bedroom window. Before sunrise they start, squawking and cawing as they fly from tree to tree, blinking shadows against the gray sky. Their numbers seem to be multiplying, especially as towns and forests overtake old farms where once crows were banished. Crow hunting peaked in the middle of the last century, but declined after crows became federally protected in 1972. Now, their omnipresence demands a new perspective; resolving our relationship with crows may take us a long way toward accepting our place in nature.

September 21

Crows seem particularly symbolic this time of year. Maybe it is the way their plumage shines like midnight in the afternoon, or the way their conversations send burnished leaves drifting to the ground; or perhaps it's their hunger for the fruit now being harvested in the fields. With breeding season over, crows once again congregate in roosts of a dozen, a hundred, a thousand birds. Before heading to the roost to sleep, crows gather in a different place an hour or so before nightfall, where they call out, chase each other, and fight. Ted Williams wrote in *Wild Moments*, "Even when we persecuted crows, we admired them for qualities we saw in ourselves. American crows are aptly named. They belong in and to our land. They are loud, resourceful, durable, and adaptable. They live in wilderness and megalopolis, prospering with or without us. They are part of smoke-scented twilights and crisp, otherwise silent mornings, part of what we were, are, and hope to be."

Crow

September 22

The autumnal equinox occurs sometime today or tomorrow. The sun and the moon are at right angles to each other, as the sun crosses over into the Southern Hemisphere and the amount of daylight is roughly equal to the length of night.

September 23

Ravens can be distinguished from crows by their larger size and the shaggy feathers at the neck and legs. Ravens have a larger vocabulary than crows, and make a deep croak, among other vocalizations. Ravens soar high in the air, their bent, ragged wings and wedge-shaped tails recognizable. On the coast, ravens are a major predator of seabird eggs.

September 24

Black bears are beginning the feeding frenzy that will last them through hibernation. Gaining two pounds a day, bears eat enough in fall to double their weight. On the Maine coast, black bears inhabit spruce-fir forests and blueberry barrens. Black bears are rare on the coasts of New Hampshire and Massachusetts, preferring inland cornfields and oak, beech, or hickory stands during the autumn months.

September 25

Sea-run brook trout (*Salvelinus fontinalis*) are funneling into coastal streams to spawn. Sea-run trout, also called salters, are an anadromous form of the brook trout. Salters migrate to coastal waters in the spring, spending the next several months in salt water, where they grow much bigger than their inland relatives. In fall, salters enter freshwater streams to deposit their eggs in the cool, shady, gravelly sections of the riverbed. While many populations of sea-run trout have disappeared from New England's coastal rivers, salter populations continue to thrive where access to the sea has not been blocked, and where upstream habitat has been protected. On the West Coast, sea-run cutthroat trout are called "harvest trout" because they are often caught this time of year. In New England, sea-run brook trout are something of a mystery for fish biologists and a secret for anglers, who would rather not disclose the locations of their favorite salter fishing spots.

September 26
Trout that are coming inland from their days at sea may pass striped bass heading in the opposite direction. This time of year, stripers are leaving the larger rivers of the Northeast to spend the winter off the mid-Atlantic coast, in Delaware and Chesapeake bays. As baitfish move, so do the stripers, bunching up and organizing to chase the small fish as a group, driving them into tidal bays and up onto the flats.

September 27
For some adult yellow eels who have been living in lakes and rivers for the last ten or fifteen years, the call of home can no longer be denied. The eels transform into migratory "silver eels," and their skin thickens and takes on a bronze-black sheen. Then, when rivers and streams are swollen from heavy autumn rains, they wait for a moonless night to leave their freshwater residences and make the long journey back to the Sargasso Sea. Eels return to the place of their birth to spawn and die. How they are able to complete the journey is still unknown, but it is possible that they use their sense of smell to detect chemical clues that help them navigate from rivers to the sea and back again. Eel populations are declining all over the world, prompting concern from scientists and river advocates. We should all be concerned, as eels are one of our great animal mysteries, and we have much to learn from their experiences traveling across entire oceans.

September 28

The inevitable fall rainstorms that signal eels to migrate play a major role in the ocean food web. Flooded rivers and streams pour large amounts of fresh water, nutrients, and organic matter into the Gulf of Maine. The nutrients fuel blooms of phytoplankton.

Rachel Carson wrote of the fall phytoplankton in *The Sea Around Us*: "Autumn comes to the sea with a fresh blaze of phosphorescence, when every wave crest is aflame. Here and there the whole surface may glow with sheets of cold fire, while below schools of fish pour through water like molten metal."

Often the autumnal bioluminescence is caused by dinoflagellates that are multiplying furiously in a short-lived repetition of the spring blooming. Unlike the spring bloom, which progresses up the Gulf from south to north, the fall phytoplankton bloom begins in the northern Gulf and spreads southward. Along the Downeast and Maritime Canada coasts, the spring and fall blooms are so close together that they are actually one bloom with a peak in midsummer. Blooms happen in spring and fall because that is when the ocean is mixing and both nutrients and light are available. During summer and winter, layers of ocean water are at different temperatures, and as the colder layers sink, the ocean becomes stratified, preventing light and nutrients from circulating.

September 29

The autumn plankton blooms provide fuel to migrating fish and other animals. Striped bass and eels have left. The herring, signaled by cool and shortening days, gather for their final spawning event of the year. Dogfish and mackerel make an encore appearance as they pass through near-shore waters on their migration south. Lobsters move to deeper water.

September 30

It seems as if the entire coast is preparing for the coming winter. Such mental and physical preparation is crucial for survival. But we also must remember that fall is a short season, and we should take time to bask in the sparkling sunshine and autumnal colors, to enjoy the fruits of the harvest season, to take long walks in comfortable weather.

ALL MORNING

All morning the rambunctious boats
that are learning to be boats
circle the harbor,
At each turn they hold on tight
as if in jeopardy—
each error a correction.

From the land
the humans are not visible. The boats
take turns being leader.

I love the bonding together
in the service of water—

as water releases them.

Kathleen Ellis
Orono, Maine

October

Frost Leaf

October 1

As the autumn morning dawns, each stem and leaf is rimmed with frost, lending a silvery hue to the day's first light. The sun takes longer to reach a height from which it can burn through the stubborn fog that hovers over the sea. The voice of the wind gathers strength. The fiery hues of autumn will soon fade to Earth's more subtle tones—but let us not think of what lies ahead, for now flames of color are reaching their full intensity, fish are on the move off the coast, life is quickening in celebration of the season past and preparation for the one ahead.

October 2

Blustering winds that send dry leaves skittering like crabs across the beach are a reminder that October is the end of hurricane season. The largest storms on Earth, hurricanes originate in the warm waters of the tropical Atlantic. When the ocean reaches 80°F (26.6°C), warm, moist air evaporates from the sea surface. As the rising air cools, water vapor condenses, releasing energy that drives the formation of thunderstorms. The Coriolis forces of the spinning earth cause the storms to rotate counterclockwise. Continued heat and moisture fuel the spiraling cyclone, which achieves hurricane status when winds are sustained at 74 miles per hour. If conditions are right, the hurricane will be forced north by westerly winds as it travels toward the East Coast of North America. Most direct hurricane hits in New

Skittering Leaves

England occur on the southern coasts of Connecticut and Rhode Island or Cape Cod; under a unique set of circumstances, a hurricane could land around Boston or the Casco Bay region. More often, New England receives the soaking rains and winds that are the leftovers of hurricanes that landed elsewhere. Perhaps the greatest threat to our coast is flooding from storm surge, a wall of water pushed toward shore by an approaching hurricane. When the strong winds of a hurricane move over the Gulf of Maine, they churn up cooler water from below, and after a storm passes, the sea surface temperature can be lower by several degrees.

October 3

Henry Bryant Bigelow was born on this day in 1879 in Boston, Massachusetts. Bigelow is considered the father of modern oceanography, in part because he took an ecosystem view of oceanography as a combination of different scientific disciplines: in trying to understand the oceans, we must view them as a zoologist, a botanist, a chemist, a physicist, a geologist, and an archaeologist. In 1912, Bigelow began a twelve-year intensive study of the Gulf of Maine, during which he collected enough data to describe the fish, plankton, and physical oceanography of the Gulf. He wrote *Fishes of the Gulf of Maine* with William C. Schroeder in 1925. He went on to become a professor at Harvard University and the first director of the Woods Hole Oceanographic Institution and the inspiration for the Bigelow Laboratory for Ocean Sciences. His research continues to be relevant for those studying the circulation and biology of the Gulf of Maine.

October 4

One of the fish that Bigelow described is the Atlantic cod, the manifest species of New England. In the Gulf of Maine, cod begin spawning in winter (although some do spawn in fall in the Bay of Fundy and waters to the east) and the eggs hatch weeks later. The larvae drift around in the upper layers of near-shore waters for several months. When they have grown to over one inch long, they settle to the bottom for the autumn months. Here they are vulnerable to predators and fishermen's nets unless they quickly find shelter in crevices and between rocks.

October 5

Thoughts of autumn are not complete without reflecting on the changing leaves. Biologist Bernd Heinrich has said that leaves are solar panels, because they make energy from sunlight. As trees and shrubs stop producing food in their leaves, they have no need for chlorophyll, which begins to break down. Green gives way to yellow and red, pigments that are always in the leaf, but are normally overwhelmed by more plentiful green chlorophyll. Other conditions including temperature and weather can hasten or delay the color change, and temperature fluctuations cause chemical changes within the leaf itself that can fade or strengthen color hue and brightness. Unlike in summer, when sunshine seems to pour all around us from above, the selective autumn sun falls at angles, and in the cooler weather we notice where it is not: the northern and eastern-facing trees are the first to change color, and northeastern beaches are cast in shadow, forcing us to seek out southern shores for refuge from the approaching cold.

Red Maple

October 6

Some of the first trees to change color are red maples, especially in swamps where they are stressed by waterlogged conditions and shallow roots. Now blazing scarlet, red-maple swamps are easily the most common freshwater wetland in New England. Red maples (*Acer rubrum*) are versatile, aggressive trees that can grow in a variety of settings. In swamps, red maple trees often have multiple trunks and easily sprout from stumps. Once you have located a stand of red maples from their autumn color, take note of the location so you can watch for the trees again when they flower in the spring.

October 7

In a subtle echo of the crimson maples, cranberries are ripening in coastal bogs, the cool fall nights turning the berries a dark ruby red. The American or large cranberry (*Vaccinium macrocarpon*) is a low, creeping evergreen vine that grows in freshwater bogs and other acidic waters of the Northeast. Cranberries have been used for centuries, first by Native Americans and later by American whalers and mariners, who carried the vitamin C-rich fruit on their voyages to prevent scurvy. Cranberries also have a long history of cultivation, beginning in 1816 when Captain Henry Hall of Dennis, Massachusetts, became the first to successfully cultivate cran-berries. The cranberry is one of North America's three native

fruits that are commercially grown (blueberries and Concord grapes are the others). Each year, farmers harvest cranberries from over 250 acres in Maine and 14,000 acres in Massachusetts. To find them in Maine, head east to Washington County and look for bogs among the spruce trees. In Massachusetts, duck behind the Provinceland dunes, where secret pitch pine forests in the slacks are carpeted with mats of giant cranberries. The low areas behind the dunes intercept the lens of fresh water trapped beneath the sand, providing ideal growing conditions for cranberries.

October 8

The award-winning poet Philip Booth was born in Hanover, New Hampshire on this day in 1925. His mother was a native of Castine, Maine, and the Booth family spent their summers on that Penobscot Bay peninsula. Booth moved to Castine in the 1980s and continued to write about the coast and its people. He passed away from complications of Alzheimer's disease in 2007.

October 9

Cued by the waning light of day, hormonal changes in plant cells bring about senescence, botany's poetic term for death. Leaf drop in deciduous trees and shrubs begins with chemical changes in the plant's cell walls and the release of hormones that trigger the disintegration of cellulose. The weakened plant fibers are easily broken by the wind, the leaf falls, and scar tissue covers the exposed surface where the leaf detached. The plant continues to redirect its energy and nutrients to stem and roots, as dead leaves collect on the ground. Autumn's heavy rains wash the leaves into coastal streams, where they become food for a number of scraping, chomping, and grazing insects and their larvae. These aquatic animals break down the rich carbon food source in the leaves into smaller and smaller pieces, which the current brings to more hungry animals that wait downstream. The insects and other invertebrates become food for fish and amphibians, and thus the leaves that today scatter from the terrestrial treetops will become part of a new food web in our rivers, connecting land to water, mountain to sea.

October 10

Viewed from a boat out on the water, the changing leaves are even more prominent against the coast, which is cloaked in the dark shades of evergreens. Deciduous trees lose their leaves as a strategy to reduce the need for water during the winter when the ground is frozen and water supplies are low. But this strategy also means that the tree has to produce new leaves in the spring, which requires considerable nutrients and energy. Instead of dropping their leaves, evergreens reserve their energy and cope with low nutrient supplies by holding on to their needles. They do slow down, however, and only produce food on days when the sun is warm enough to stimulate photosynthesis.

October 11

There is an exception to this strategy among the evergreens. The larch, also called tamarack or hackmatack (*Larix laricina*), is a coniferous softwood tree that loses its needles in fall and produces new ones each spring. Larches are easily spotted now, as they stand like yellow candles in wooded swamps and bogs.

Tamarack

Clusters of yellow needles burst from the ends of small, warty spurs on the branches. The tamarack is a northern tree that ranges as far south as New Jersey and Pennsylvania. Its wood has been used for poles, posts, and railroad ties, and its seeds, needles, and inner bark are eaten by grouse, snowshoe hares, red squirrels, porcupines, and deer. The larch grows in wet soils, which forces the roots to grow at right angles to the trunk. As a result of this phenomenon, larch were used to create "knees" used for shipbuilding.

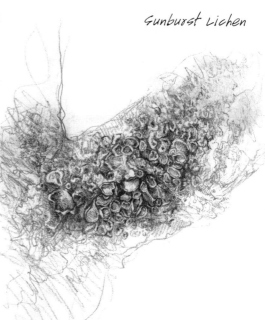

Sunburst Lichen

October 12

The yellow-orange of changing leaves is mirrored by the orange splotches on rocks, trees, fenceposts, and gravestones near the ocean. These orange spots are actually crusts of the maritime sunburst lichen (*Xanthoria parietina*). This flat, leafy lichen may form a distinct narrow band on rocks just above the high-tide line. Lichens are actually two separate organisms, a fungus and an alga, living together in a symbiotic relationship: the fungus gets food from the photosynthesizing alga, and the alga is able to survive in a dry environment, protected by the surrounding fungus. Lichens obtain nutrients and water directly from the atmosphere, a feature that makes them sensitive to air pollution.

October 13

Joining the conspicuous yellows of larch and lichen is the witch hazel (*Hamamelis virginiana*), a shrub or small tree that waits to bloom until after the leaves have fallen. Yellow, spider-like flowers emerge from the branches in late fall, filling the woodland understory with a yellow haze. The distilled extract of witch hazel bark and leaves is an astringent long used for a variety of medicinal purposes. Witch hazel grows throughout the Northeast and along the southern coast of Nova Scotia.

Witch Hazel

Bur Oak Acorn

October 14

While in the woods searching for witch hazel, you may hear a crunching of acorns underfoot. The fruit of oak trees, acorns are a rich food source that ensures the survival of many species of wildlife. Oak (*Quercus* spp.) is an uncommon tree of the coastal zone, except for the pitch pine–oak forests of Cape Cod, south-eastern Massachusetts, and southern Maine. Bear or scrub oak is a thicket-forming shrub or small tree that grows in rocky or sandy soil along the southern New England coast; the under-sides of its leaves are covered with whitish hairs. Two of the white oaks, which have leaves with rounded lobes, prefer wet-lands and grow in coastal areas: swamp white oak, considered a species of special concern by the Maine Natural Areas Program, and the mossycup or bur oak. In floodplain forests and wetlands around Penobscot Bay, you may chance to encounter the tiny fringed acorns of the mossycup oak.

October 15

The October full moon is the Hunter's Moon, rising early and casting light onto prey that are now easily seen through bare branches, a signal that hunting season has arrived. The harvest is in, moose and deer are fat and on the move, and food is need-ed for the winter. Populations of moose and deer on the coast have fluctuated with civilization. For example, when Europeans first colonized Maine, white-tailed deer (*Odocoileus virginianus*) occurred only in the midcoast and southern parts of the state; the vast interior forests north and west were occupied by moose and caribou. Deer populations expanded over the next 200 years as forests were cleared and major predators such as the wolf were extirpated. Wildlife managers have had varied success moving deer around the coast. In the mid-1950s, a group of deer were moved from Swan Island in the Kennebec River to Monhegan Island. The deer did well, and island residents hunted them in the fall, after summer tourists had left for the season.

However, habitat destruction and Lyme disease began to take their toll on the island, and the deer were removed in the 1990s. Both moose and deer are good swimmers, and they periodically show up on coastal islands; a few of Maine's larger islands like Mount Desert seem to support resident moose populations, and deer swim back and forth to islands that are close to shore.

October 16
When a black-legged kittiwake is seen from the coast, winter cannot be far behind. A medium-sized gull, the black-legged kittiwake (*Rissa tridactyla*) spends most of its time at sea. It is the only gull able to dive underwater for fish and to follow ships across great bodies of water; the kittiwake ventures far when other gulls stay close to shore. Kittiwakes arrive in autumn after leaving their summer breeding grounds in the Canadian Maritimes, where they build nests of seaweed and guano on rocky cliffs. In Nova Scotia, they are called fall gulls. Look for them now as they soar above the coast, at first seeming like the more common herring gull but soon distinguishable by their white wings tipped in black. Or listen for their shrill cry— *kitte-wa-aaake!* Soon they will travel farther across the Gulf, dominating the skies above Stellwagen Bank and Jeffrey's Ledge.

Black-legged kittiwakes

October 17
In another aerial reminder of the season, great southward-pointing arrows of Canada geese are moving overhead. Although there are also resident, nonmigrating Canada geese, the North Atlantic *Branta canadensis* flying over us are just passing through on their migration from Labrador to New Hampshire's Great Bay or coastal Massachusetts, or points further south. In October, migrant geese may join resident flocks for a meal or two. Before 1960, there was not a breeding population of Canada geese in Maine; their numbers have increased over the last 50

Canada Geese

years, and today they can be found throughout the state. Other geese that may be spotted migrating through New England are the snow goose, white-fronted goose, and Atlantic brant.

October 18

Wet summers mean lots of fat insects, which means food for spiders, because if insects thrive, spiders thrive. With the leaves off the trees, spiders are more noticeable, and many are at their fattest right now. Maine has at least 600 species of spiders; none are truly poisonous, though most can bite. Some spiders are more visible during the fall because they go ballooning: a spider positions itself atop a plant, then releases strings of silk from its rear, which catch the wind, carrying the spider off to a new home. E. B. White gave us our best description of launching spiders in *Charlotte's Web*. Silken strands of a thousand spiders shimmer in the morning dew. Still other spiders are making their annual attempt to stow away in woodpiles or get through cracks in the house searching for a warm place to spend the winter. While humans have invented plenty of synthetic fibers over the last 150 years, we have never been able to replicate spider silk, one of the toughest fibers around.

October 19

Now, when the moon is waning and rising later in the evening, a new ocean of stars spreads across the southeastern sky: Capricornus, the sea goat. Aquarius, the water bearer. Piscis Austrinus, the southern fish. Pisces, the fishes. Cetus, the whale (sometimes called the sea monster). Eridanus, the river. Watch them ebb and flow as night carries on. This dimly lit part of our night sky, with its elusive constellations, is sometimes called the Celestial Sea.

October 20

Much more prominent is the constellation Orion, which now begins to dominate the northeastern horizon. In Roman mythology, Orion was sometimes said to be the son of Neptune, god of the sea (Poseidon, to the Greeks). Orion was a great hunter, as was Diana, whom he was about to marry. Diana's brother, Apollo, did not want her to marry Orion, but she wouldn't listen. One day, observing Orion wading far into the ocean with just his head above the water, Apollo pointed it out to his sister and maintained that she could not hit that black thing on the sea. The archer-goddess discharged a shaft with fatal aim. When Orion's body washed ashore, Diana, bewailing her fatal error with many tears, lifted Orion to the sky, placing him among the stars. Forevermore, Orion stands watch in the winter sky, seeing us through until the spring. To find him, look for the three bright stars in a line that make up his belt; his bow and arrow can be seen above the belt to the right.

Orion

October 21

This is surely Orion's time to shine, for the meteor shower that bears his name occurs in mid- to late October. Meteor showers are named for the area of the night sky where they appear to originate, which is known as the radiant. To see October's Orionid meteors, face the southern horizon and watch for swift streaks of light that seem to emanate from his left shoulder. These shooting stars are really remnants of Halley's Comet, the bits of ice and rock left behind as the comet makes its seventy-six-year orbit around the sun. It is because of the earth's tilt and rotation that we are able to view the comet's path this time of year. The comet itself was last visible from earth in 1986, and will return in 2061.

October 22

"Now, once again, the Hunter rose to drive summer south before him, once again autumn followed on his steps. I had seen the ritual of the sun; I had shared the elemental world. Wraiths of memories began to take shape. I saw the sleet of the great storm slanting down again into the grass under the thin seepage of moon, the blue-white spill of an immense billow on the outer bar, the swans in the high October sky, the sunset madness and splendour of the year's terns over the dunes, the clouds of beach birds arriving, the eagle solitary in the blue. And because I had known this outer and secret world, and been able to live as I had lived, reverence and gratitude greater and deeper than ever possessed me, sweeping every emotion else aside, and space and silence in an instant closed together over life. Then time gathered again like a cloud, and presently the stars began to pale over an ocean still dark with remembered night."
—Henry Beston, *The Outermost House*

October 23

Back on Earth, time moves much faster. Autumn is brief, and all too soon the winds carry only the smell of decay: leaves rotting in the streams, frozen seaweed drying on the beach, spruce and pine sealing their cones with resin. Everything is sticky, brittle, wet and dry at the same time. After summer's heady intensity and the plenty of the harvest, the smell of fall is welcome. It is comforting to know that as we feel the urge to slow down, to rest, to be warm, so too the earth is digesting a full season and storing energy for the months to come.

October 24

Follow the cold, briny smell to the marsh, where among the stems of spartina are the reddish bunches of *Salicornia*, the glasswort. Glasswort, sometimes called samphire, has plump, green, succulent stems that absorb salt and water, and turn red in fall. Glasswort grows in the transition zone between the high marsh and the low marsh; it is edible, lending a salty crunch to salads. One species of moth feeds exclusively on *Salicornia*. And one species of *Salicornia*, the dwarf glasswort, is designated by the State of Maine as a rare species of special concern. Dwarf glasswort is found in southern Maine, where it reaches its northern limit.

October 25

The first oceangoing ship built by European colonists in America, the pinnace *Virginia*, was constructed in October 1607 at the Popham Colony at the mouth of the Kennebec River. While the settlement lasted only a year, the 50-foot, 30-ton *Virginia* was a major accomplishment. It marked the beginning of the shipbuilding industry on the Kennebec River, and proved that a colonist-built vessel could range the coast of Maine and make several transatlantic voyages.

October 26

Schools of fat Atlantic mackerel, *Scomber scombrus*, are leaving their spawning and feeding grounds in the Gulf of St. Lawrence, rippling across the surface of the Gulf of Maine as they move to warmer waters near the edge of the continental shelf. They will stop when they reach water warmer than 45°F (5°C), somewhere off the coast of North Carolina. Mackerel are in the same family as tuna and swordfish. Their velvety backs are greenish-blue with dark bars, their bellies silvery white. Henry Bigelow said that the mackerel's "iridescent colors fade so rapidly after death that a dead fish gives little idea of the brilliance of a living one," an apt metaphor for fall, when the brilliantly colored leaves, once fallen, fade to dull browns, and the bleached marshes turn to straw. By the end of December, schools of mackerel will have vanished from the coast, and won't return until spring.

Atlantic Mackerel

October 27

Following the mackerel south may be pods of harbor porpoises, members of the toothed whale family. Others move offshore to avoid advancing ice cover during winter. For example, Bay of Fundy porpoises have been observed off the New Hampshire coast in winter, suggesting that some populations have limited seasonal migrations. Harbor porpoises (*Phocoena phocoena*) range the northern seas around the globe; in the western Atlantic they favor coastal shelf waters from Labrador and the Bay of Fundy south to North Carolina. A harbor porpoise has a short, stocky body that is dark gray above and white underneath. There is a dark stripe from the mouth to the flippers, and a small, triangular dorsal fin. They are not that easy to spot: they surface for short, quick periods and then dive for several minutes. The harbor porpoise can sometimes be detected by its sharp, puffing, sneezelike blow. The best place to see them is from a high cliff above calm seas. Harbor porpoises are vulnerable to shipping traffic and entanglement in fishing gear.

October 28

Time is running out. All that is left of the foliage are fading flames of gold atop the birches, and gilded tamaracks tarnishing in the cold, damp air. While it seems there are more leaves on the ground than on the trees, all is not lost. For there, on the tips of most deciduous trees and shrubs, are the buds of next year's green. Summer's sunlight and drenching rains have provided the trees with enough energy to form their buds, and they enter the dormant season well-prepared for spring. Find a way to make yourself so prepared, so you, too, can enter winter with the comfort of knowing you already hold the key to unlocking spring.

Sea Smoke

October 29

If the days are cold enough, clouds of smoke may hover over
the sea like steam above a witch's cauldron. Really plumes of
fog that form when cold dry air meets warm moist air over
the ocean, sea smoke appears in autumn and early winter when
arctic air rolls off the continent onto warmer Atlantic waters.
The air above the water is warmer and lighter than the polar
air, and drifts upward. As the air rises, water vapor condenses
into small visible droplets, like your breath on a cold day, and
columns of sea smoke sway above the sea. Eventually, columns
of sea smoke may collapse into a layer of thick fog.

October 30

On the eve of Halloween, a frightening and monstrous fish
lurks in the deep waters of the ocean, ready to eat unsuspecting
prey from the inside out. The hagfish, or slime eel (*Myxine
glutinosa*), is one of the oldest marine creatures. Hagfish use
smell to find food, usually marine worms in the mud but
occasionally fish, which the hagfish bores into, using a sharp,
toothed tongue to tear apart the inside of the fish. After such a
large meal, the hagfish may not eat again for months. Hagfish
are covered with slime glands that can emit a gallon of slime
at once; they use this slime as a defense mechanism against
predators. Hagfish flesh is eaten in Asia, and the skin is used
to make "eelskin" wallets, shoes, and other products.

October 31

The desire to become something other than ourselves is not a purely human trait; animals wear costumes, too. By blending into their surroundings, fish avoid being eaten and are able to sneak up on unsuspecting prey. Bottom-dwelling fish like winter flounder can change color from reddish-brown to grayish-green to almost black, depending on the color of the seafloor. And then there is the decorator or spider crab (*Libinia emarginata*), perhaps the most garish of the costumed sea creatures. As the decorator crab wanders around the ocean, it blends in with its surroundings by wearing them: the crab attaches to the outside of its shell anemones, corals, seaweed, algae, and whatever else is lying around.

DEER ISLE

"Mostly," he said,
"people leave. The
ones that stay are
likely a little odd.
We get some summer
folks, of course.
But when the snow
comes, they go."

Above us, a rattle
of leaves, as up
through the birches
bursts a swirl of
starlings, late,
heading south.

Burt Hatlen
Orono, Maine

November

November 1

November arrives like the first scratch of wool on unseasoned skin. Stems of frost heave from the earth during the long cold night, and at dawn melt back into the not-yet-hardened earth. Leaves are down, nuts are stored, fishes and birds are on their way south. The harbors begin to empty, save for a few scallop or lobster boats. For those who stay, life becomes a pursuit of comfort, and a withdrawal. Each of us has our own rituals to prepare for winter. But November is more than preparation; it has its own celebrations and observances, if only we would stop and look.

November 2

The fastest time for sailing across the Atlantic is thirteen days, one hour, and twenty-five minutes, a record set in 1854 by the *Red Jacket*, a Maine-built clipper ship. *Red Jacket* was ornate and graceful in addition to being fast. A life-sized figurehead of the Seneca chief occupied the bow, and gold-leaf scrollwork decorated the stern. Rosewood, mahogany, black walnut, and more gilt work finished the interior, which could house a sixty-two-man crew. Named for the Seneca Indian chief Red Jacket (a nickname for the ever-present British red coat he always wore), the 251-foot, 2,400-ton clipper was launched at Rockland, Maine on November 2, 1853. The following January, she left New York on course for England. Captain Asa Eldridge of Yarmouth,

Downy Woodpecker

Massachusetts, sailed through snow, hail, and rain, and arrived in Liverpool Harbor less than two weeks later. Red Jacket remains one of the fastest sailing ships in history.

November 3

With most of the leaves down, holes in trees become more noticeable. Who made those holes? A woodpecker, probably. The downy woodpecker makes perfectly round holes in dead trees. The pileated woodpecker, our largest red-headed woodpecker (which looks much like the cartoon Woody Woodpecker), makes large oval or rectangular holes up to five inches across. The pileated's large beak leaves a pile of wood chips and shavings at the base of the tree. Later, flying squirrels may take up residence in the holes the pileated woodpecker leaves behind. The yellow-bellied sapsucker drills small holes in rows or rings around the trunk of a live tree and waits for sap to run out, then laps it up along with any insects that get stuck. Instead of making holes, the black-backed woodpecker strips away patches of bark to expose juicy grubs underneath. The black-backed woodpecker does excavate a small hole in a dead tree when nesting. You, too, may feel the urge to "hole up" when the autumn winds turn blustery, carrying a hint of winter on their breath.

Pileated Woodpecker

Eagle Nest

November 4

Nests are also more noticeable this time of year. The most
visible are large clumps of leaves, which are squirrel nests.
Now that the forest canopy is transparent, it may be easier to
spot the large nests of bald eagles, constructed of sticks, twigs,
leaves, mulch, and other found materials. Eagles return to the
same nest year after year, enlarging it each nesting season.
Look for them in tall pine trees along large rivers and estuaries.

November 5

The rumors of snow that drift across coastal bays are forcing
horseshoe crabs to contemplate hibernation. Along much of the
East Coast, horseshoe crabs migrate out to the relatively warmer
waters of the continental shelf for the winter. In Maine, the
Taunton Bay population stays put, hunkering down in the mud
at the edges of deeper channels, where they hibernate for six
months, sometimes beneath thick layers of ice, before emerging
in late spring to breed. The Taunton Bay horseshoes are the
northernmost documented breeding population in North
America.

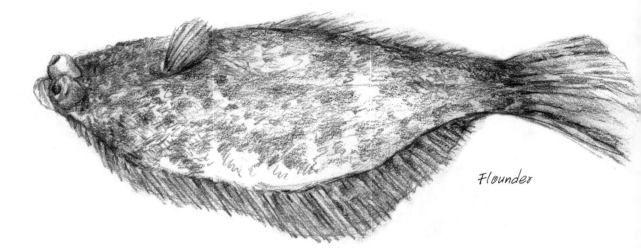

Flounder

November 6

While many species are preparing for their dormant phase, winter flounder (also called lemon sole or blackback flounder, *Pseudopleuronectes americanus*) are moving into shallow harbors. Spawning will occur later in the winter and early spring, near the mouths of estuaries. Winter flounder are born symmetrical, with eyes on both sides of their heads, and swim like other fish. As they grow older, the left eye migrates to the right side and the body flattens to take on the familiar flounder appearance. Antifreeze in their blood allows them to survive the winter, and they can change color to match their surroundings. Our other flounders, both with their eyes to the left, include the summer flounder and the more round-shaped windowpane flounder— with skin so thin you can almost see through it.

November 7

Soft-shell clams (*Mya arenaria*) and other bivalves can also handle the freeze, although they grow slowly or not at all from late fall through the winter. While we usually think of clams as a summer treat, many of our diving ducks—like goldeneyes, eiders, and black ducks—rely on young clams and other mollusks for food during the winter. The young clams, which settle to the mud flats in late summer and early fall, can only burrow as deep as their breathing siphon is long, which is not very far, making them easy prey for ducks. To sustain natural populations of this valuable and tasty resource, the Downeast Institute for Applied Marine Research and Education raises millions of baby clams each year at its Beals Island hatchery, near Jonesport, Maine. The cultured clams are planted, or "seeded," on mud flats around the state. Although the cultured clams are as hardy as their wild counterparts and could survive freezing winter temperatures, the clams can get scoured or moved by ice, or eaten by ducks. So Brian Beal, a professor of marine ecology at the University of Maine at Machias, and his staff hold the tiny clams—only a centimeter long—at the hatchery over the winter, and then transplant them onto mud flats in the spring. This ensures that, come summer, there will be plenty of fried clams available.

Hoarfrost

November 8

After a cold, clear October night, look outside for leaves that wear a coat of shattered glass, and twigs laced with frozen air. This is hoarfrost, which forms when water vapor turns directly to ice. Water droplets suspended in the cold air freeze when they come in contact with a cold surface; branches, objects, and even the ground may be covered with delicate white ice crystals in the form of needles, platelets, ferns, or feathers.

November 9

While endangered northern right whales should have headed south weeks ago, in some years they linger in bays and near-shore waters into November. When this happens, lobstermen and other fishermen are put on alert to watch out for the whales. In some cases, the fishing season is delayed until the whales decide to move out. Despite their eagerness to get to work, fishermen are part of a network of people who look out for the whales and help protect them.

November 10

November allows for that northern quality of light, when the shallow rays of the sun cut through the forest, illuminating the rocks and moss and shape of the landscape, brighter, open, and clear, the light illuminating individually that which is but part of a whole the rest of the year. Gone is the collective green; in its place are bark and roots of individual trees. Of the November atmosphere, Henry Beston wrote, "Now comes November and a colder sky with a prophecy of winter in its lessened and russet light, and something of the vast silence of winter in the air." The beaches are quiet, the skies are empty but for crows and shadows and the last arrows of geese, and even the sea seems to be withdrawing. Yet in the seeming emptiness, the subtleties of sea and sky can breathe, and be, as can we.

November 11

Step outside to greet the northern sky, where the water meets the clouds. Now that our star stays low and the atmosphere is growing colder, sundogs may appear on clear, cold days. Sundogs—mock suns, or parhelia—are bright spots to the left and right of the sun. Ice crystals falling from high clouds refract the sun's rays, forming bright spots as they pass on either side of the sun. Sometimes the sundogs look like patches of rainbow, adding the color of ice-shine to the ceiling of our shore.

November 12

Though we may have lost its true meaning, Indian summer still brings warm, hazy days to give us a brief respite from the oncoming cold. Maybe the haze was smoke from the burning grasses or forest floor being cleared by Native Americans. Or maybe the haze was dust and dirt in the air from forests being cleared for farms by colonists. Or maybe the settlers of New England were observing the natives leaving their villages this time of year, moving to inland areas where winter conditions were more favorable, especially for hunting bear, caribou, moose, and deer. Thoreau called Indian summer our finest season of the year; at the very least, it is the finest *time* of the season.

November 13

The full moon in November is the Frost Moon because, well, there is plenty of frost around. It is also called the Beaver Moon, signifying the last chance to set beaver traps before rivers and swamps freeze over, in order to ensure a supply of warm and valuable furs for the winter. This time of year, beavers (*Castor canadensis*) are busy building their dams higher in order to raise water levels. A larger flooded area allows the beavers to access fresh trees and transport gnawed pieces to repair the lodge and dam, or to store as food. The larger the beaver colony, the more food that is needed and the deeper the water needs to be to provide access to it. The underwater food pile can grow as large as four feet high and 20 feet across, enough to feed an adult male and female as well as their one- and two-year-old offspring through the winter. The beavers swim under the ice from their lodge to their food supply. Today, beavers are much more common than they were a century ago because fewer are being trapped and because our forests are shifting toward more hardwood species like aspen and birch, the beaver's favorite foods. While beaver dams can create problems, they are a natural part of the landscape and have been for centuries. As they go about the business of creating, abandoning, and reforming flooded areas, beavers act as habitat engineers, allowing new soil to form and new plants to grow, providing food for other wildlife. And unlike most of the dams we build, a beaver's dam is only temporary.

Beaver

Jack Pine

November 14

As evergreens become more noticeable against the ever-dulling
landscape, Indian summer's warm days are good times to
search for Maine's lesser-known pine trees. Unlike the
famed white pine, which has bundles of five needles, red
pine and jack pine have only two needles per bundle. Red pine
(*Pinus resinosa*), also called Norway pine, has soft, dark-green
needles four to six inches long and yellowish-red bark. Red pine
grows throughout the Gulf of Maine region, along the coast and
the western mountains. Red pine is often used in reforestation
and plantation sites. Jack pine (*Pinus banksiana*) has short
(one to two inches), stiff, yellow-green needles. The curved
cones remain attached to the tree for many years, until a fire
comes along to create the heat necessary to open them. Being a
fire-loving tree, jack pine can tolerate drought and grows in
sandy, acidic soil. Mountain slopes in Acadia National Park are
good places to look for jack pine.

November 15

At night, when cold and clear, another gift from the universe
may be received in November: the Northern Lights. *Aurora
borealis* begins as a solar flare or other explosion that sends
particles of the sun into space. As the particles approach Earth,
they run into our magnetic field, and are directed to the northern and southern ends of the planet, where they release their
energy as photons of light only visible to those of us who live
in or near polar regions. Around the world, the Northern Lights
have been described as an ocean afire, or the reflection of schools
of herring, perhaps because only the sea could rival a hundred
thousand pieces of the sun crashing into Earth, colliding with
our atmosphere in curtains of shimmering, ethereal light.

Red Pine

November 16

Against an overcast sky, the bare branches of a yellow cherry tree are strung with tiny sour moons. Cries of blue jays overlap with the dry howls of sea gulls. A crow hides among sprays of fir, squirrels make tracks in the frost. Sea gulls poke at empty plastic containers in the parking lot. What has brought them so far inland? Certainly not the shores of this pavement sea. No, gulls are intelligent and adaptive, just like us. They are carnivores and scavengers, like us, and they flourish in the landscapes we have created: landfills and dumpsters, fish piers and picnic grounds. They will steal your sandwich while you're taking a swim in the ocean. They will pick the wrapper clean and beg for more. Can we blame them? There are fewer fish in the ocean for birds to eat, less coastal land available for their nests. Gulls will fly 30 or 40 miles inland to eat, returning to the coast to sleep at night. Herring gulls (*Larus argentatus*) and great black-backed gulls (*Larus marinus*) are our most common species. Herring gulls are white with a gray back, black wingtips, and a yellow beak. Brownish-white gulls are immature herring gulls. They steal and scavenge around human settlements, and also hunt live prey. They pick up mollusks in their beaks, fly over a hard surface, and drop them from above to crack open the shells.

Herring Gull

The number of gulls using inland sites, especially during migration and winter, has increased. Natural sources of food in inland areas do not exist during the winter in Maine; the gulls are here because of us. Wherever you see great swirling eddies of gulls in the sky, you find the refuse we call trash and gulls call food.

Winterberry Holly

November 17

The ripe red fruits of the winterberry holly (*Ilex verticillata*) still cling tightly to their branches. You can see them now, scarlet clumps in swamps and roadside ditches. The winterberry, also called black alder, is inconspicuous most of the year, a simple shrub or small tree with green leaves. A native deciduous holly, winterberry grows in wetlands throughout the eastern U.S. Songbirds feast on the berries, and by midwinter most branches of the winterberry will be empty, so enjoy them now. They are a reminder that each species has its moment in the sun, its turn in the seasons.

November 18

Now that the days are getting shorter and we are in Eastern Standard Time, you may be rising earlier to catch as much sunlight as you can. Several places in Maine lay claim to being the first place in the United States to see the sunrise (although no doubt it is the fishermen at sea who see it first, no matter the season or location). In fact, the honor depends on the time of year, as sunrise moves from south to north to south. At this time of year, Cadillac Mountain in Acadia National Park is the first to see the sun. Once March rolls around, sunrise will first cast light upon East Quoddy Head, at the easternmost end of the country—but only for a month, after which Mars Hill in northern Maine receives first light until September; then East Quoddy gets another month of the honor until November.

November 19

The Leonid meteors streak through the eastern night sky in mid-November, appearing to emanate from the constellation Leo, which appears over the Gulf of Maine above the eastern horizon. The Leonids are fast—traveling toward Earth at 158,000 miles per hour, they are the trail of cosmic debris left behind by the comet Tempel-Tuttle, which passes by earth every 33 years.

November 20

Those drab little birds
darting into the waves
below the wrack line of dead
grass might be dunlins. The dunlin (*Calidris alpina*), gray above and
white below in winter, has black legs and a long
black bill that it uses to probe the shallows and mud
flats for tiny crustaceans, insects, and fish. In summer it can
be distinguished by its black belly. Also called a fall snipe,
the dunlin has a later migration than most shorebirds, moving
through Maine in October and November on the way to
wintering areas to the south. They sometimes form large flocks.
In flight, the dunlin shows a white bar on each wing, and its call
is a high-pitched trilling *kreeee!*

Dunlin

November 21

When waters turn suddenly cold in late fall or early winter,
marine turtles, stunned by the chill, may get stranded on beaches.
The loggerhead, with its reddish-brown carapace outlined in
yellow, must leave the North Atlantic before the water temperature dips below 50°F (10°C), or it may become cold-stunned and
hypothermic. The same is true of the Atlantic or Kemp's Ridley
turtle. The loggerheads and Ridleys will not return to our waters
until early summer. In contrast, the leatherback, the world's
largest turtle, is not affected by cold temperatures. Leatherbacks
follow the migration of jellyfish, their favorite food, which
thrive in the sheltered, nutrient-rich waters of the Gulf of
Maine. By autumn, leatherbacks are chasing jellyfish south
through the bays and sounds of New England.

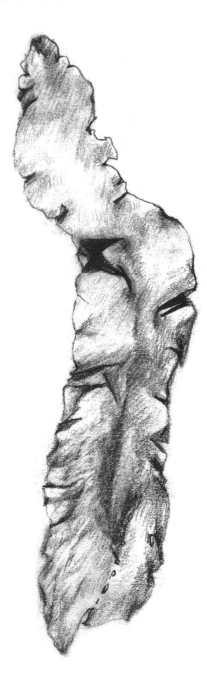

Porphyra

November 22

While it seems that most of our plants have disappeared and
nothing is growing, one need only look to the edge of the sea
for new life. Several species of red algae in the genus *Porphyra*
are just now appearing below the high-tide line on exposed and
semiexposed rocky shorelines. *Porphyra linearis* has narrow
straplike fronds that grow in the upper intertidal zone. During
low tide, the dark brown and purple pigments allow the large
algae to absorb the sun's rays and keep from freezing. Look
for it now; by March, the delicate blades will have vanished,
replaced by other species of seaweed.

November 23

The air above the Gulf of Maine is beginning to cool, but the sea
is still holding on to summer's warmth. The Gulf is stratified:
warmer, lighter water floats at the sea surface; below this warm
layer is water that is still as cold and salty as it was in winter.
This difference in temperature and density fuels the counterclockwise circulation of the Gulf of Maine, and these currents
are now at their widest and fastest. Soon the atmosphere will
have cooled enough that the surface of the ocean also cools. As it
cools, it sinks, and the layers mix together. The currents slow down,
and by February, the counterclockwise circulation pattern is no
longer evident. The currents will not start spinning again until
spring.

November 24

As the Gulf of Maine currents reach the end of this year's spin
cycle and ice begins to form on the edges of tidal rivers, boats
begin their retreat from the water. Yachts are sheathed in their
white plastic cocoons, stacked in storage yards of marinas up and
down the coast. Docks are pulled from the water and piled on
shore. Canoes and kayaks are stashed in barns and garages until
spring ice-out. A few motorboats remain active, ready for early

morning duck hunting and island hopping between neighbors. And many fishing boats are getting tuned up for a busy season —hearty lobstermen set traps amid the ice and snow, scallop and urchin divers begin braving the icy depths, and still other fishermen have yet to begin their season. Seafood is a year-round business in the Gulf. The ocean never sleeps, and neither do we who live at the ocean's edge. The ocean provides; we are thankful.

November 25

Our winter visitors have been arriving, those birds escaping Arctic regions for the relative warmth of the Gulf of Maine coast. They are only here for a few months, and are worth finding. Why not go to the Penobscot River or the Harraseeket to see Barrow's goldeneyes? A few hundred leave their nests in lakeside trees in Labrador and the Gaspé Peninsula to spend time in our unfrozen coastal rivers. The Barrow's goldeneye (*Bucephala islandica*) has a glossy black head with a white crescent in front of the yellow eye, black above and white below; they sometimes mingle with their cousins, the common goldeneyes. They stay on the river, diving to the bottom for food, until ice forces them to move out to saltier waters. If you catch them on the move, you may hear their wings whistling in flight, or catch a glimpse of white patches on their wings.

Barrow's Goldeneye

November 26

Loons are usually solitary birds, haunting wild ponds through-out the North. But come autumn, loons young and old gather on large lakes in preparation for their winter migration to the sea. Disguised in their washed-out whitish-gray plumage, they take off, the adults usually ahead of the young. They are destined for points south and east, for bays, coves, channels, inlets, and other shallow areas off the coasts of Maine, New Hampshire, and Massachusetts. Some travel as far as Mexico. Common

loons (*Gavia immer*) will spend the next few months on
unfrozen waters, eating flounder, rock cod, menhaden, sculpin,
and crabs. They stay close to shore, diving 10 to15 feet below
the surface to find food. Silhouetted against the gray November
waters, cormorants, mergansers, and grebes can be mistaken for
loons—but the loon looks heavier, and holds its black bill more
horizontal than the others. Also, the red-throated loon is arriving
from the Arctic, and as both loons begin to molt into their dull
gray winter plumage, they will be difficult to tell apart.

John James Audubon called the common loon the great
northern diver: "I have met with the Great Diver, in winter, on
all the water-courses of the United States, whence, however, it
departs when the cold becomes extreme, and the surface is con-
verted into an impenetrable sheet of ice. I have seen it also along
the whole of our Atlantic coast, from Maine to the extremity of
Florida, and from thence to the mouths of the Mississippi, and
the shores of Texas, about Galveston Island, where some individuals in the plumage characteristic of the second moult, were
observed in the month of April 1837. Indeed, as is the case with
most other species of migrating birds, the young move farther
south than the old individuals, which are better able to withstand the cold and tempests of the wintry season."

Common Loons

Young loons will wander the coast for up to seven years before picking a territory and settling down; the adults will return to their same lake each summer to breed. Seeing a loon on the coast is a reminder of how the mountains are connected to the sea, how inland life is drawn to the edge, and, when returning, brings the ocean to the mountain.

November 27

On this day in 1898, the *SS Portland* left Boston headed for Portland with 192 passengers on board. The steamship hastily departed port, hoping to beat an approaching storm, but instead crossed paths with one of the most famous northeasters of all time. The *Portland* attempted to turn around and return to Boston, but could not outrun the storm. She sank about 20 miles north of Cape Cod.

Winter Loon

November 28

While technically it is still autumn, November truly is the beginning of winter in the Gulf of Maine. The daylight hours dwindle to nine; the temperature dips below freezing. Storm tracks intensify, as the jet stream slips south, driving cold rains out of the St. Lawrence River Valley and over New England. From the east, strong winds move up the coast, throwing waves at the empty beaches and pushing the tide higher. The term "northeaster" reappears in our vocabulary, and some of the biggest rainstorms of the year occur. All of this rain brings the rivers up close to flood stage, and replenishes groundwater supplies before everything freezes.

November 29

Most of our annual plants along the shore—those that die each fall and grow back from seed in the spring—are brown, brittle, and broken. One of these is wild rice, an important plant for Native American cultures, although it is less common along the East Coast than elsewhere. To find it, launch your boat on the Cathance River in Bowdoinham, Maine, and head downstream to Merrymeeting Bay. If you go now, you may run into the writer Franklin Burroughs on a duck-hunting excursion. Burroughs wrote of the wild rice, "On the Bay, long mats of dead and sodden stems are drifting back and forth on every tide by mid-November, and if you walk along the beach at Popham, where the Kennebec empties into the sea, you will find windrows of them as flotsam along the dune line." Mixed in with the dead stems are seeds of next year's plants, which will sprout in spring after spending the winter buried in mud and ice. Wild rice (*Zizania aquatica*) is a tall grass with full, heavy heads of seed that wave in the marshes like grain in the fields of America's breadbasket.

November 30

The poet Leo Connellan was born on this day in 1928 in
Portland, Maine. Connellan grew up in Rockland, a bittersweet
experience that stayed with him even after he settled in
Connecticut as an adult. Maine remained a "lifelong quarrel"
that played out in his poems. He wrote, honestly and unroman-
tically, of lobstering and clam factories, blueberries and boats
adrift in an unforgiving sea, as in the poem "Maine":

Autumn hauls
bright Fall to brown dust. The sea
changes its colors at whim yet can
hit beaches furious, drawing back to strike.
The human here is lost in survival isolation.

Wild Rice

SEASCAPE

This is the captured product
of no artist's fevered hand,
of no ground pigment,
or brush-stroked hope.
Paint-hazed chips of ocean,
blunted by a fog-gift day,
rise and fall against an
imagined beyond;
impressionist fulfillment
is in the feathery pines
made abstract by a loving eye.
Is there a soul
whose anxious fear is not
washed away by pulsing tide
and beaded fog-damp hair,
And then brought back—
heightened—by
the keening human gulls?
Time-ground sand is wet,
and the massive rocks are waiting.

Gus Bombard
Old Town, Maine

December

December 1

"No one goes until everyone goes." That's the motto on December first, or the first good-weather day after today, which is trap day on Monhegan. A small island 10 miles off the coast of Maine, Monhegan closes its waters to lobster fishing from May through November, a self-imposed rule that the state legislature formalized in 1998. Trap day is a big day, but the lobstermen will wait until everyone is ready. The islanders help each other with repairs and bringing traps down to the docks, and soon the water for two miles around the island will be peppered with lobster buoys.

December 2

For other lobstermen, who would rather not fish during the cold, dangerous winter season, now is a time for fixing gear and painting lobster buoys. A single lobsterman could have anywhere from 60 to 600 buoys, all of which need to be painted a certain way so that he (and other lobstermen) can identify a trap as his own. Every lobsterman registers his color pattern and each buoy bears his license number.

December 3

By this time of year, lobster pounds have reached their maximum capacity. Pounds are areas of shallow water in which lobstermen hold live lobsters to keep the supply—and prices—steady.

Mermaid's Purses

Lobsters are placed in pounds in the fall, allowing them a few months to acclimate to the new environment; the cool water prevents disease and provides plenty of oxygen to the lobsters, but from now on, water temperatures in pounds will be too cold for new lobsters to adapt. Pounds are usually located in closed-off areas near shore; the first lobster pound was created on Vinalhaven Island in 1875.

December 4

As the temperature of the ocean drops, some fish move offshore to deeper waters where the temperature does not fluctuate, and others move inshore to shallow waters that warm in the pale winter sun. The winter skate moves into shallow areas of gravel or sandy bottom, from Canada to North Carolina. Winter skate is one of seven species of skates occurring along the North Atlantic coast (the others are the barndoor, clearnose, little, rosette, smooth, and thorny). Winter skates (*Leucoraja ocellata*) are large animals that can live up to 20 years. Skates are responsible for so-called mermaid's purses—the hard, black, leathery egg cases with long horns on each corner that wash up on the beach like so many tiny sleds entangled in dry rockweed strands.

December 5

Another fish only just arriving is the Atlantic tomcod (*Microgadus tomcod*). The tomcod ranges in coastal near-shore waters from Labrador and Newfoundland to Virginia, preferring the mouths of brackish streams, estuaries, and muddy harbors. Tomcod are also known as frostfish because they run up rivers to spawn during the frosty months of December through February. They feed mostly on small crustaceans (especially shrimp and amphipods), worms, small mollusks, squid, and juvenile fish. The anadromous tomcod lives in the chilly shadow of its more famous marine kin, the cod.

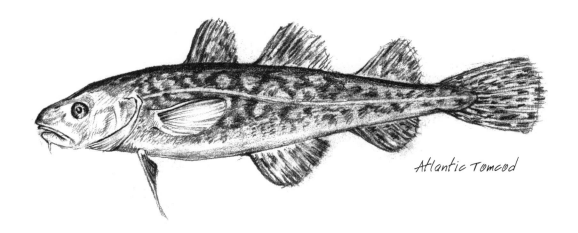

Atlantic Tomcod

December 6

Photographer Eliot Porter was born on this day in 1901.
The Porter family summered on Great Spruce Head Island in
Penobscot Bay, Maine, where, among sweet fern and bunchberry,
bay and twin flower, a young Eliot Porter found "the tonic of
wildness." Trained as a scientist but driven as an artist, Porter
photographed the landscape of New England: lichens on stone,
fog-shrouded spruce, fish houses, and jetsam cast upon the
beach. His photos are rich with color and detail, yet somber
as a winter's day.

Rainbow Smelt

December 7

At six to eight inches long, rainbow smelt are the smallest
of our anadromous fish, and now they are moving into
estuaries where they will spend the winter. Ice shacks may
appear on the ice above them as fishermen begin the traditional
winter harvest of *Osmerus mordax*. Come spring, the smelt will
chase the thaw upstream to spawn in freshwater rivers. Smelt
feed on zooplankton, shrimp, worms, and smaller fish; they in
turn are eaten by striped bass, bluefish, and birds. They travel
in schools in shallow water less than a mile from shore.
Commercial landings of smelt peaked in 1966 at 360,000
pounds, with the majority being taken from Maine waters.

Ice-Fishing Shack

Atlantic White Cedar

December 8

Pollock begin spawning in shallow waters of the Gulf of Maine, especially along Jeffrey's Ledge and the eastern slope of Stellwagen Bank, at the mouth of Massachusetts Bay, and north to Isles of Shoals and Casco Bay. The young pollock (*Pollachius virens*) that are born in the winter sea will disperse throughout the Atlantic, from the Gulf of St. Lawrence to New Jersey, and occasionally as far south as North Carolina. The name of the Passamaquoddy Tribe of Native Americans means "those who pursue the pollock," and their tribal home on Passamaquoddy Bay between Maine and Canada is the "pollock-plenty-place."

The pollock is deep olive-green with a silvery-white belly and a sharp silver line running down each side. Also called Boston bluefish, saithe, coalfish, or green cod, the pollock is an important food fish caught in the same nets as cod and haddock. While it is often grouped with these groundfish, pollock live anywhere from rocky bottoms to near the ocean surface, and they will gather by the hundreds in great schools. Pollock are voracious eaters, hungry for small fish, shrimp, and other crustaceans. As they move closer to shore for spawning this time of year, they are more frequently caught, and are a favored target of sport fishermen. Oceanographer Henry Bigelow noted their capacity to fight, and that they will take an artificial fly ("silver body with white wings of hackle or hair is good, especially with a touch of red") or bite on clams or small baitfish.

December 9

Lobster buoys used to be made out of cedar but today are mostly styrofoam. Atlantic white cedar (*Chamaecyparis thyoides*) grows in forested swamps near the coast. The northernmost stand is in Appleton Bog in midcoast Maine. Saco Heath, Maine, Rye, New Hampshire, and Cape Cod, Massachusetts, are other good places to see this uncommon tree, which looks similar to northern white cedar, or arborvitae, but with narrower, less-flattened foliage. In a typical Atlantic white cedar swamp, trees form a dense canopy that blocks out sunlight, limiting growth in the understory. The wood and crushed leaves are fragrant, as are the tiny, waxy blue fruits. Hessel's hairstreak is a tiny green-and-brown butterfly that lives exclusively in Atlantic white cedar swamps; females lay their eggs on cedar leaves. The light-weight, durable wood was used in shipbuilding—hence the nickname "boat cedar"— and as shingles. Because of its value as lumber (and development pressure on the coastal plain), Atlantic white cedar has disappeared from many areas.

Snowflake

December 10

The first snow may or may not have fallen; whenever the first white falls, we seem to be so much more impressed than with mere rain. A speck of dust high above the sea begins to fall. As the tiny particle moves through a cloud (which itself is but a swirling mass of water droplets), it attracts molecules of water. If it is cold enough, the accumulating water molecules will form ice crystals around the particle, now a snowflake. The exact arrangement of the crystals depends on the temperature and humidity of the air, and no two snowflakes are alike. Once snowflakes hit the ground, they immediately begin to lose their shape. Snow over the ocean melts upon contact, a microscopic act of dilution. Each snowflake is like a Tibetan sand mandala, an intricate work of love and art, only to be dismantled upon completion. What is the lesson here? Surely there is one of individuals, and of community, for once the snowflakes land they become snow, a blanket, a cover for the earth until spring, a collective warmth that brightens the surrounding world. In one year, approximately 92,366 *cubic miles* of water enter the ocean as rain or snow. Before this freshwater input can drive the ocean's conveyor belt of circulating currents, it begins as solitary rain drops or mandalas of crystallized water.

December 11

What about snow *in* the ocean? "Marine snow" is a term
that describes bits of decomposing plants and animals that fall
through the water column of the sea, settling to the bottom.
As these particles drift to the ocean floor, whole communities of
bacteria gather upon them, munching away on the carbon and
other nutrients that are part of the snow. Marine bacteria, which
are the oldest living organisms on Earth and collectively represent
the largest biomass in the ocean, have evolved to respond very
rapidly to marine snowstorms, gravitating toward areas of heavy
particle settling and forming colonies of chemical deconstruction.
By ripping the snow particles apart, the bacteria make energy
available for the rest of the food web. Marine snow can often
be seen as white or grayish specks in underwater videos and
photographs.

Marine snow is made of particles that are large enough
to penetrate "the ocean's veil," the network of microorganisms
that stretches through the water surface. Smaller particles are
consumed by the bacteria, viruses, and tiny protists that make
up the veil. These organisms swim through the ocean's sunlit
layer, which seems thick as honey because the organisms are
so small. This universe of the microbial food web is still being
explored, but scientists believe the ocean's veil influences the
ecology, chemistry, and climate of the sea.

December 12

December's full moon is the Cold Moon or the Long Night
Moon. The normal daily average temperature in December
is 26.5°F in Portland and 33.6°F in Boston. The record low
temperature for this month in Portland is -21°F; in Boston, -7°F.
Most nights get below freezing, and the nights are longer since
we're approaching the solstice.

December 13

Fishermen take advantage of December's long nights by taking care of tasks that get neglected during the harvest season, like painting buoys and mending nets. In the 1930s, before the days of high-tech gear and modern fishing methods, a fisherman spent one-fifth of his income on nets. Washing, drying, mending, and airing nets took up a lot of time. Nets, once made of Irish linen, then cotton twine, now plastic and synthetics, are still very much a part of fishing, and fishermen still experiment with new net styles, mesh sizes, and shapes for the most efficient catch. The phrase "mending the nets" means putting something in working order again.

December 14

The Geminid meteor shower peaks around this time, and it is often the best light show of the year. Other meteor showers like the Perseids and Leonids have been lighting up the night sky for hundreds or even thousands of years. The Geminids are more recent, appearing suddenly in the mid-1800s and becoming more intense over the years. And unlike meteor showers of previous months, which are the debris shed by comets when they get near the sun, the Geminids are caused by Phaethon, an extinct or dormant comet that has accumulated a thick crust of interplanetary dust grains, which gives it an appearance more like an asteroid. The thick pieces of dead comet that fall toward Earth from the direction of the constellation Gemini are slower, and tend to leave brighter, longer, and more graceful streaks in the sky.

Gemini

December 15

Winter is shrimp harvesting season, which usually runs from December to April. The shrimp caught here are northern shrimp (*Pandalus borealis*), which live in arctic and subarctic waters; the Gulf of Maine is the southern extent of their range. The northern shrimp is pinkish to red, between three and five inches long. In winter the females migrate inshore to areas with soft, muddy bottoms to drop their bluish-green eggs before returning to deeper offshore waters for the summer. The northern shrimp fishery is now considered sustainable, thanks to rebuilding stocks and the introduction of the Nordmore grate in 1992, a device attached to shrimp nets that greatly reduces by-catch of species like sea turtles. Shrimp season is a welcome holiday, since it represents the availability of fresh, locally grown food at a time when the fields are dormant and we are back to eating from cans and jars. Northern shrimp are the sweetest, tenderest shrimp of all.

December 16

On this day in 1866, astronomers at an observatory in Calais, Maine, marked the passage of stars above their heads, completing the connection between time in Greenwich, England, and time in North America. With the successful laying of the Trans-atlantic Telegraph Cable in July of that year, observers with the Coast Survey were able to use the telegraph to record the time span between when a star passed over Calais and when the same star passed over the next astronomical station to the west. Since the earth rotates 360 degrees each day (24 hours or 1,440 minutes), the time difference between the two observatories reveals how many degrees separate them—and so time becomes space and our longitudinal position on the face of the globe could be determined.

December 17
The sun that brief December day
*   Rose cheerless over hills of gray,*
*   And, darkly circled, gave at noon*
*   A sadder light than waning moon....*
—John Greenleaf Whittier

John Greenleaf Whittier was born in Haverhill, Massachusetts, on this day in 1807 and spent most of his life in the Merrimack River Valley of northeastern Massachusetts. Whittier was one of New England's best-known poets, but he was also a newspaperman and an abolitionist with political aspirations. It was in his later years that Whittier turned to nature and drew upon his experience growing up on a working farm to write his best work. John Pickard writes in *American Writers*, "The romance that he found in these familiar things was based on an awareness that humble experiences and simple feelings possessed as much wonder and beauty as any dream."

December 18
The sea urchin fishery peaks from now through February. Urchins may be harvested by diving, raking, trapping, or dragging. Divers collect urchins with gloved hands, placing them into mesh bags. A handful of licensed fishermen stand on rocky shores and comb the seafloor with long-handled rakes. When urchins are plentiful, lobstermen notice that their traps become covered with what to them are spiny pests, but urchiners realized they could simply use baited crates thrown into kelp beds to catch the critters. Most urchins are taken by draggers, using a modified scallop dredge to scoop the echinoderms off the ocean bottom.

December 19

When the Japanese depleted their local urchin stocks and began looking for new supplies in the 1980s, Maine fishermen quickly jumped at the chance to participate in a new and profitable fishery. In what is now considered a classic boom-and-bust situation, within five years the fishery went from almost nonexistent to the second most valuable fishery in the state after lobsters. Landings peaked in 1993 and have declined every year since.

With hundreds of tube feet, sea urchins shimmy across the seabed in search of kelp, their favorite food, but they can survive on other kinds of macroalgae and small animals. Sea urchins once dominated the seafloor in many areas of the Gulf of Maine, fouling lobster traps and devouring kelp so that entire kelp forests disappeared. The barren seafloor became covered with coralline algae, and the urchins, going hungry, were smaller and grew slowly. Eventually, with fewer urchins around due to the fishery of the 1990s, kelp beds returned. Over three million pounds of urchins were harvested from Maine waters in 2006.

December 20

Cold cannot hurt this country huddled under hemlock;
It ekes out cover of a kind, what with spruce and fir
And threadbare birch and alder. This chill means snow;
But fields are ready for it, they are not caught napping
Though the sun goes wan now, skimmed over like the pools.

This is an excerpt from a poem by Abbie Huston Evans, who was born on this day in Lee, New Hampshire, in 1881. She moved to Camden, Maine, when she was a teenager, where she met fellow writer Edna St. Vincent Millay. Evans lived in Philadelphia as an adult, but continued to spend her summer vacations in Maine. Her first book of poetry, *Outcrop*, with a forward by Edna St. Vincent Millay, was published in 1928. Millay wrote, "These are poems of one more deeply and more constantly aware than most people are, of the many voices and faces of lively nature." Evans's poetry is a world where oysters are the true philosophers, and men can learn to live on seedpods left above the snow, like the birds in winter:

Oh make me honest as a fishing village
In the full sun-glare on a northern coast:
As honest as a hill above bare tillage
When leaves are down and cliffs and scars show most!
How long till snow? How long?

December 21
Winter solstice occurs when the sun reaches its lowest point in the sky, creating the longest night and shortest day of the year in the Northern Hemisphere.

December 22
Come away! come away! there's a frost along the marshes,
And a frozen wind that skims the shoal where it shakes the dead black water;
There's a moan across the lowland and a wailing through the woodland
Of a dirge that sings to send us back to the arms of those that love us.
—Edwin Arlington Robinson

Today is the birthday of Edwin Arlington Robinson, born in the village of Head Tide, Maine, in 1869. His family later moved to Gardiner on the Kennebec River, a typical American boom town with industries in lumber, ice, shipping, and manufacturing. He was awarded the Pulitzer Prize for poetry three times, in 1922, 1925, and 1928.

December 23

"The mountains everywhere piling up out of the sea, mountains tumbling over and into one another with curious shapes and most wonderful islands, severe, rocky, forbidding, beautiful."

Artist John Marin wrote these words upon seeing Mount Desert Island for the first time. Marin was born on this day in 1870 in New Jersey. He first came to Maine in 1914 and spent almost every summer thereafter on the Maine coast, painting in and about Small Point on Casco Bay, and later in Stonington on Deer Isle. In 1933, Marin spent his first summer at Cape Split, near Addison, Maine. The following year, he bought a house there, where he would spend summers for the rest of his life.

December 24

Like the tomcod and winter skate, the smooth flounder (*Liopsetta putnami*) breeds in estuaries in winter, a habit that earned it the nickname "Christmas flounder." Perhaps these fish have evolved to release their eggs during the cold winter months to give their offspring a jump-start on life.

December 25

Every year, millions of people will go outside today and count the number and types of birds they see as part of the annual Christmas Bird Count. The National Audubon Society started the count in 1900 as an alternative to duck hunting, the traditional family holiday activity at the time. The count actually runs between December 14 and January 5, and the data are used by biologists to track populations of birds around the world.

December 26

An uncommon bird of the Christmas Bird Count is the scaup. Two similar-looking species of this diving duck are found in the Gulf in winter: the greater scaup (*Aythya marila*) and the lesser scaup (*Aythya affinis*). Both have white sides and black heads, but the greater scaup is a bit brighter white and is slightly larger with a more rounded, greenish-black head. The lesser scaup is one of the most abundant and widespread of the diving ducks in North America. Lesser scaup feed primarily on animal life. Greater scaup feed on both plant and animal life, especially clams. Populations of both scaups have declined significantly over the past 20 years, especially in their breeding grounds in the boreal forest of western Canada.

December 27

A frequent winter visitor to the exposed, ice-free rocky coast and stone jetties of the Gulf of Maine is the purple sandpiper (*Calidris maritima*), also called winter bird, winter peep, winter rockbird, and winter snipe. The purple sandpiper, slate gray with a slight purplish tint, is larger and fatter than other sandpipers, with a long, drooping bill. They are often seen in flocks. They are tame, but will fly low over the water when flushed. Come spring they will follow the winter as it retreats north, nesting on the edges of the snowy and ice-bound Canadian Arctic.

December 28

Maine artist Andrew Wyeth said, "I prefer winter and fall, when you feel the bone structure of the landscape—the loneliness of it, the dead feeling of winter. Something waits beneath it, the whole story doesn't show." Winter is a time to look at the bones of the landscape, the shapes of trees and the slope of the land and the way shadows follow paths of ancient glaciers. Rocks you never noticed stand front and center, waiting for you to find the whole story that waits beneath the season.

Purple Sandpiper

December 29

Now that the trees are bare and the sun is low, the belt of Venus may appear. Named after the Roman goddess Venus, the belt is a pink, purple, or brownish border just above the dark shadow of the horizon, separating earth from the sky above. The purplish haze is visible all around you, not just in the direction of the sunset. It is most visible when the atmosphere is cloudless, yet very dusty, just after sunset.

December 30

The counterclockwise gyre of currents in the Gulf of Maine reaches its broadest extent and greatest speeds by the end of December. Then, cooling of the atmosphere results in cooling of the ocean surface. As it cools, it sinks, replacing the stratified layers with well-mixed waters. As the currents in the Gulf mix downward, they are slowed by the friction they encounter when they reach the bottom. By February, the counterclockwise circulation pattern will no longer be evident.

A similar process happens in large, deep lakes, which also stratify during the summer. As water temperatures in the surface of the lake cool in fall, the layers mix and the lake "turns over." When lakes freeze over, temperature and oxygen levels are similar at all depths.

December 31

New Year's Eve, and the year ends as it began, in winter. On this last day of the year, look back at all that has happened in the world around you over the course of a year in the Gulf of Maine, and how much more remains unknown. For even now, after all these words, we can ask, as Rachel Carson did,

"Who has known the ocean? Neither you nor I, with our earth-bound senses."

January 1
Remarks of the president on the occasion of the dinner given by Sir Howard Beale, ambassador of Australia to the United States, Newport, Rhode Island, September 14, 1962.

January 4
Burlingame, R. 1958. "Marsden Hartley's Androscoggin: Return to Place." *New England Quarterly*, 31 (4): 447–62.

January 8
National Marine Fisheries Service commercial landings statistics for Maine, Massachusetts, and New Hampshire, 2006.

January 11
MacDonald, C. 2004. "Freezing Point of Sea Water." Hook, Line and Thinker (*The Newsletter of the Fishermen and Scientists Research Society*), 3, Halifax, Nova Scotia.

January 13
Maine Geological Survey, Surficial Geologic History of Maine, www.maine.gov/doc/nrimc/ mgs/explore/surficial/facts/surficial.htm
Fletcher. 1993. General Geology of Barnstable County, Massachusetts. Soil Survey of Barnstable County, Massachusetts. http://nesoil.com/ barnstable/barngeology.htm
Oldale, Robert N. 2001. Geologic History of Cape Cod, Massachusetts. U.S. Geological Survey, Woods Hole, Massachusetts.
http://pubs.usgs.gov/gip/capecod/index.html

January 16
Dean, D. 1978. "Migration of the Sandworm Nereis virens During Winter Nights." *Marine Biology*, 45:165–73.

January 18
From "Birches" in *Modern American Poetry* (L. Untermeyer, ed.), 1919. New York: Harcourt, Brace and Howe.

January 19
From "MS. Found in a Bottle," in the *Collected Tales and Poems of Edgar Allen* Poe, 1992. New York: Modern Library.

January 23
Cartwright, D. E. 1999. *Tides: A Scientific History*. Cambridge, United Kingdom: Cambridge University Press.

January 28
Mittelhauser, G. H., J. B. Drury, and P. O. Corr. 2002. "Harlequin Ducks (Histrionicus histrionicus) in Maine, 1950–1999." *Northeastern Naturalist*, 9:163–82.

February 12
Maine Geological Survey. 2007. Portland Tide Gauge and Waterfront, Marine Geology Field Locations, Augusta, Maine. http://www.maine.gov/doc/nrimc/mgs/explore/ marine/sites/mar07.htm

February 13
From Longfellow's poem "A Psalm of Life" which appeared in his first book of poetry, *Voices of the Night*, published in 1839.

February 14
Byron quote from *Childe Harold's Pilgrimage* (1812).

February 16
Gilbert, J., *et al.* 2005. "Changes in Abundance of Harbor Seals in Maine, 1981–2001." *Marine Mammal Science*, 21 (3): 519–35.

February 21
Zielinski, G. 2003. *Maine Climate Newsletter*, February. Orono: University of Maine.

February 22
Millay quote from "Exiled," in *Second April* (1921).

February 27
Longfellow's "Sound of the Sea" was published in *Masque of Pandora and Other Poems* (*A Book of Sonnets*) (1875). See also http://www.hwlongfellow.org/poems_front.php

February 28
From "Snow-Flakes," in *Birds of Passage* (*Flight the Second*) (1863).

March 3
Trembanis, A. C., O. H. Pilkey, and H. R. Valverde. 1999. "Comparison of Beach Nourishment along the U.S. Atlantic, Great Lakes, Gulf of Mexico, and New England Shorelines." *Coastal Management*, 27: 329–40.

March 5
See Rachel Carson, *The Sea Around Us*, p. 111.

March 7
Storm surge definition from the National Hurricane Center, NOAA. http://www.nhc.noaa.gov/HAW2/english/storm_surge.shtml

March 8
Percy, W. 1987. *The Thanatos Syndrome*. New York: Farrar, Strauss.

March 11
For reference to Artemidorus, see Lewis, D. P. 2005. "Owls in Mythology and Culture." The Owl Pages, http://www.owlpages.com/
Snowy Owl, see Speck, F. G. 1935. Mammoth or "Stiff-Legged Bear." *American Anthropologist* 37: 159-163.

March 26
Robert Frost quotes from *Steeple Bush* (1947).

March 27
Anderson, D., *et al.* 2007. Red tides in western Gulf of Maine project data. Woods Hole, Massachusetts: U.S. Geological Survey.

March 28
Length of bloom, see "Ecosystem Advisory for the Northeast Shelf Large Marine Ecosystem." *Northeast Fisheries Science Center, Advisory 2007-1.* http://www.nefsc.noaa.gov/omes/OMES/spring2007/adv6.1.1.html

April 5
From *The Waste Land* (1922).

April 6
Lobster survival rate from unpublished report of the Zone C Lobster Hatchery. Stonington, Maine: Penobscot East Resource Center.

April 12
Wind speed record information from the Mount Washington Observatory, North Conway, New Hampshire.

April 15
Smith, C. 2006. "Distribution of Vertical Lines from the Maine Lobster Fishery." Augusta, Maine: Department of Marine Resources.

April 16
Whale species in Gulf of Maine from Provincetown Center for Coastal Studies.

April 19
Payne, R. S., and S. McVay. 1971. "Songs of Humpback Whales." *Science*, 173 (3997): 585–97.

April 21
Gisel, B. J., ed. 2001. *Kindred and Related Spirits: The Letters of John Muir and Jeanne C. Carr.* Salt Lake City: University of Utah Press. See also http://www.sierra-club.org/john_muir_exhibit/

April 22
Philips, T. 2000. "Moonlit Meteors." *Science@NASA*, April 18. http://science.nasa.gov/

April 30
Jin, D., E. Thunberg, and P. Hoagland. 2006. "Economic Impact of the 2005 Red Tide Event: Project Description and Some Preliminary Results." Woods Hole, Massachusetts: MIT Sea Grant College Program.

May 1
Neely, K. K. 1956. "Study of MAYDAY and SOS as Radiotelephony Distress Signals." *Journal of the Acoustical Society of America*, 28 (4): 554–55.

May 15
Gibbs, J. P., S. Woodward, M. L. Hunter, and A. E. Hutchinson. 1988. "Comparison of Techniques for Censusing Great Blue Heron Nests." *Journal of Field Ornithology*, 59 (2):130–34. Inland migration information, personal communication with Tom Hodgeman, Maine Department of Inland Fisheries and Wildlife, August 22, 2007.

May 22
Black Bear Assessment and Strategic Plan, Maine Department of Inland Fisheries and Wildlife.

May 25
From "Nature" (1836).

May 26
Bohren, C. G. 1987. *Clouds in a Glass of Beer.* New York: Wiley.

June 2
Teale, Edwin Way. 1951. *North With the Spring.* New York: Dodd Mead.

June 9
Milewski, I. 1995. *Island Journal*, vol. 13. Rockland, Maine: Island Institute.

June 15
Clampitt, A. 1997. *The Collected Poems of Amy Clampitt.* New York: Knopf. See also the Amy Clampitt Fund, http://www.amyclampitt.org/index.html

June 16
Daley, B. 2003. "Sea of Glass." *Boston Globe*, July 13, 2003, p. B1.

June 21
Farnsworth Art Museum. 2004. *Seeing Red: Rockwell Kent and the Farnsworth Art Museum.* Exhibition catalog, September 5–November 28, 2004. Rockland, Maine: Farnsworth Art Museum.

June 22
Because our calendar is not aligned with the lunar cycle, the date of the full moon fluctuates from month to month and year to year. This book uses the full moon schedule for 2008. Full moon dates for future years are available from NASA at http://sunearth.gsfc.nasa.gov/eclipse/phase/phases2001.html.

June 26
Ross, M. R. and R. C. Biagi. 1991. *Recreational Fisheries of Coastal New England.* Amherst, Massachusetts: University of Massachusetts Press, pp. 185–89.

June 29
Celia Thaxter. 1873. *Among the Isles of Shoals.* Boston: Houghton Mifflin.

June 30
Conkling, Philip. 1981. *Islands in Time.* Rockland, Maine: Island Institute.

July 2
Census of Marine Life, Gulf of Maine.

July 4
U.S. Fish and Wildlife Service. 1997. Guidelines for Managing Fireworks in the Vicinity of Piping Plovers and Seabeach Amaranth on the U.S. Atlantic Coast. http://www.fws.gov/northeast/pipingplover/fireworks.html

July 7
Redfield, A.C. 1972. Development of a New England Salt Marsh. *Ecological Monographs*, 42: 201-37.

July 12
Thoreau, H.D. 1866. *Cape Cod*. Boston, Massachusetts: Ticknor and Fields.

July 14
Steneck, R.S. 1986. "The Ecology of Coralline Algal Crusts: Convergent Patterns and Adaptive Strategies." *Annual Review of Ecology and Systematics*, 17: 273–303.

July 18
Freshwater input from Hurricane Isabel, from presentation by A. DeCharon, Center for Ocean Sciences Education Excellence, School of Marine Sciences, University of Maine, February 9, 2007.

July 21
Comments on Moore, see Thompson Gale (2007).

July 26
Connellan, L. 1999. *Maine Poems*. Nobleboro, Maine: Blackberry Books.

July 30
For industrial shellfish products, see the Fisheries of the United States annual report from the National Marine Fisheries Service.

August 1
Phippen, S. 1982. *The Police Know Everything*. Orono, Maine: Puckerbrush Press.

August 11
Bogan, L. 1968. *The Blue Estuaries: Poems, 1923-1968*. New York: Farrar, Straus and Giroux.

August 17
Shark sighting in Wells from Associated Press article in the *Bangor Daily News*, Bangor, Maine, August 30, 2004.

August 24
Blueberry acreage in Maine from the University of Maine Cooperative Extension.

September 2
Ames, T. 1996. *Island Journal*, vol. 14. Rockland, Maine: Island Institute.

September 20
Wang, B. 2006. "Crafty Crows Keep Hunters on Their Toes." *Maine Sunday Telegram*, Portland, Maine, September 3, 2006, p. B4.

September 24
Massachusetts Department of Fisheries and Wildlife and Maine Department of Inland Fisheries and Wildlife.

October 2
National Hurricane Center, NOAA. See also Zielinski and Keim (2003).

October 3
Brosco, J. P. 1989. "Henry Bryant Bigelow, the US Bureau of Fisheries, and Intensive Area Study." *Social Studies of Science*, 19 (2): 239–64. See also biography of Bigelow from Bigelow Laboratory, http://www.bigelow.org/hbbigelow_more.html.

October 5
Heinrich's comment on leaves from a panel presentation at the Society of Environmental Journalists' annual meeting, Burlington, Vermont, October 29, 2006.

October 7
Mack, S. K. 2006. "Future Rosy for Cranberry Growers." *Bangor Daily News*, Bangor, Maine, December 11, 2006, pp. B1, B5.

October 14
Coverstone, N. 1998. "The Mighty Oak: Significant to Humans and Wildlife." *Wild About Nature*, December. University of Maine Cooperative Extension, Orono, Maine.

October 15
Personal communication with Richard Dressler, Maine Department of Inland Fisheries and Wildlife, December 4, 2006.

October 16
Cooke, M. T. 1945. "The Kittiwake as a Transatlantic Bird." *Bird-Banding*, 16: 58–62.

November 2
Crowe, M. 2001. "Sharp Boats." *Fishermen's Voice*, 6 (1). Gouldsboro, Maine.

November 9
Associated Press. 2006. "Fundy Lobster Season Delayed by Winds, Right Whale Sightings." *Bangor Daily News*, Bangor, Maine, November 14, p. B5.

November 12
Thoreau quote from "Autumn."

November 13
Maine Department of Inland Fisheries and Wildlife, Outdoors Report, 10/25/06.
Vaux et al. (unpublished). Maine Aquatic Biodiversity Project report.

November 14
Manley, R. 2006. "Maine's 2-Needle Pines Take the Stage." *Bangor Daily News*, Bangor, Maine, December 2, 2006, p. C1.

November 16
Personal communication with Scott Hall, National Audubon Society/Project Puffin, January 29, 2007.

November 18
Henderson, J. S., ed. 1994. *The Maine Almanac and Book of Lists*. Topsham, Maine: Maine Times.

November 26
Audubon, J. J. 1844. *The Birds of America*. New York and Philadelphia: J.B. Chevalier. Available online at http://books.google.com/

November 30
See Sanford Phippen's introduction to *The Maine Poems* by Leo Connellan.

December 6
Porter quotes Thoreau, "The tonic of wildness"; see *In Wildness is the Preservation of the World*, selections from Thoreau and photos by Porter (Sierra Club 1967).

December 7
Smelt landings from National Marine Fisheries Service.

December 11
Smetacek, V. 2002. "The Ocean's Veil." *Nature*, 419: 565.

December 12
Temperature averages from Northeast Regional Climate Center.

December 13
Stanford, Alfred. 1934. *Men, Fish, and Boats*. Jersey City, New Jersey: Jersey City Printing Company.

December 14
Phillips, T. 1998. "The Mysterious Geminid Meteor Shower." *Space Science News*, NASA.

December 17
Excerpt from "Snow-bound: A Winter Idyll." Pickard, J. B. 1979. "John Greenleaf Whittier," in *American Writers*, Supp. 1, vol. 2, Charles Scribner's Sons, pp. 682–706.

December 19
Urchin landings from Maine Department of Marine Resources.

December 20
"Cold cannot hurt this country..." excerpted from "Frost Is on the Bunchberry"; "Honest as a fishing village...." from the poem "Invocation." Both poems from *Outcrop*.

December 22
From "The Wilderness."

December 23
Ward, M. 2003. "A Fierce and Fascinating Place: John Marin in Maine." Essay accompanying Marin exhibit at the University of Maine Museum of Art, October 2003–January 2004.

December 28
For quote, see Corn, W. R. 1973. *The Art of Andrew Wyeth*. Greenwich, Connecticut: New York Graphic Society.

December 31
Carson, R. 1937. "Undersea." *The Atlantic Monthly*, September 1937, p. 322.

Beston, H. 1948. *Northern Farm: A Chronicle of Maine*. New York: Rinehart, Holt and Winston, Inc.

_____. 1928. *The Outermost House: A Year of Life on the Great Beach of Cape Cod*. New York: Doubleday.

Bigelow, H. B., and W. C. Schroeder. 1925. *Fishes of the Gulf of Maine*. Washington, D.C.: U.S. Government Printing Office. Available at http://www.gma.org/fogm/

Burroughs, F. 2006. *Confluence: Merrymeeting Bay*. Gardiner, Maine: Tilbury House.

Burroughs, J. 1886. *Signs and Seasons*. New York: Harper and Row.

Carson, R. 1955. *Edge of the Sea*. Boston: Houghton Mifflin.

_____. 1951. *The Sea Around Us*. New York: Oxford University Press.

_____. 1941. *Under the Sea-Wind*. New York: Simon and Schuster.

Census of Marine Life, Gulf of Maine Program. 2006. Gulf of Maine Register of Marine Species. Portland, Maine: Gulf of Maine Research Institute. http://www.usm.maine.edu/gulfofmaine-census/

Coffin, R. P. T. 1949. *Coast Calendar*. Indianapolis: Bobbs-Merrill, reprinted by Down East Books, Camden, Maine, 2003.

Dillard, A. 1974. *Pilgrim at Tinker Creek*. New York: Harper & Row.

Estrin, N. B., and C. W. Johnson. 2002. *In Season: A Natural History of the New England Year*. Hanover, New Hampshire: University Press of New England.

Graham, A., and F. Graham. 1981. *Birds of the Northern Seas*. New York: Doubleday.

Haines, A. 1998. *Flora of Maine*. Bar Harbor, Maine: V. F. Thomas.

Hannah, J. 2000. *Seals of Atlantic Canada and the Northeastern United States*. Guelph, Ontario: International Marine Mammal Association, Inc.

Hay, John. 1981. *The Undiscovered Country*. New York: W. W. Norton.

Heinrich, B. 1999. *Mind of the Raven*. New York: Cliff Street Books.

Hunter, M. L., Jr., A. J. K. Calhoun, and M. McCullough. 1999. *Maine Amphibians and Reptiles*. Orono, Maine: University of Maine Press.

Jewett, S. O. 1896 (Dover Thrift Edition 1994). *The Country of the Pointed Firs*. New York: Dover Publications, Inc.

Kammen, M. 2004. *A Time to Every Purpose: The Four Seasons in American Culture*. Chapel Hill, North Carolina: The University of North Carolina Press.

Kingsbury, J. M. 1970. *The Rocky Shore*. Old Greenwich, Connecticut: The Chatham Press, Inc.

Leopold, A. 1949. *A Sand County Almanac*. New York: Oxford University Press.

Marchand, P. 2000. *Autumn: Season of Change*. Hanover, New Hampshire: University Press of New England.

_____. 1996. *Life in the Cold*. Hanover, New Hampshire: University Press of New England.

McAtee, W. L. 1951. "Bird Names Connected with Weather, Seasons, and Hours." *American Speech*, 26 (4):268–78.

McCall, R. 2006. *Small Misty Mountain: The Awanadjo Almanack*. Sedgwick, Maine: Pushcart Press.

McPhee, J. 2002. *The Founding Fish*. New York: Farrar, Straus and Giroux.

McGee, D. W. 1999. *Flora of the Northeast: A Manual of the Vascular Flora of New England and Adjacent New York*. Amherst, Massachusetts: University of Massachusetts Press.

Montgomery, S. 2000. *The Curious Naturalist: Exploring Nature's Everyday Mystery*. Camden, Maine: Down East Books.

_____. 2002. *The Wild Out Your Window: Exploring Nature Near at Hand*. Camden, Maine: Down East Books.

Northwest Atlantic Marine Alliance. 2006. "Ecosystem Relationships in the Gulf of Maine—Combined Expert Knowledge of Fishermen and Scientists." *NAMA Collaborative Report*, 1: 1–16.

Ogilvie, E. M. 1950. *My World Is an Island*. New York: Whittlesley House.

Petrides, G. A. 1988. *Eastern Trees* (Peterson Field Guides). Boston: Houghton Mifflin.

Petry, L. C., and M. G. Norman. 1963. *A Beachcomber's Botany*. Chatham, Massachusetts: Chatham Conservation Foundation.

Sarton, May. 1977. *House by the Sea*. New York: Norton.

Teal, J., and M. Teal. 1969. *Life and Death of the Salt Marsh*. New York: Ballantine Books.

Thompson Gale. 2004. *Contemporary Authors Online*. Accessed via University of Maine, Literature Resource Center database. http://www.library.umaine.edu/auth/auth.asp?db=Literature+Resource+Center

Thurston, H. 2004. *A Place Between the Tides*. Berkeley, California: Greystone Books.

Watling, L., J. Fegley, and J. Moring. 2003. *Life Between the Tides*. Gardiner, Maine: Tilbury House.

White, E.B. 1942. *One Man's Meat*. New York: Harper & Brothers.

Williams, T. 2004. *Wild Moments*. North Adams, Massachusetts: Storey Publishing.

Zielinski, G., and B. Keim. 2003. *New England Weather, New England Climate*. Lebanon, New Hampshire: University Press of New England.